THE ULTIMATE HCG DIET COOKBOOK

for

the *Revised* Simeons' HCG DIET

by Beth Golden, PhD, ND

with Special Recipe Contributions by

Chef Joseph Chouinard

DEDICATION

This book is dedicated to the 1000's of HCG dieters who helped validate the success of weight Loss with additional foods and the newly-created recipes. Their insistence on having access to a wide variety of creative and tasty, yet HCG Diet-compliant and easy-to-fix recipes while on the *Revised* HCG Diet is appreciated.

Information and recommendations presented in The Ultimate HCG Diet Cookbook for the Revised Simeons' HCG Diet are provided for informational purposes only and are not intended to diagnose or treat a disease or illness; to serve as medical advice; or as a substitute for medical treatment. Consult your Medical Doctor before beginning any weight management program

TABLE OF CONTENTS

TABLE OF CONTENTS (CONT'D)

From our KITCHEN to YOURS ...

Back in the 50s, Dr. ATW Simeons' developed a very simple list of foods to be eaten while following his HCG Diet. Through the years, variations of the actual diet have been tried but, until recently, no one has conducted research or clinical trials to prove or disprove what food modifications and / or revisions can successfully be made.

Based on our clinical research since 2007, now comes the *Revised* Simeons' Diet allowing more than 160 newly released recipes in **The Ultimate HCG Diet Cookbook for the Revised Simeons' HCG Diet.** Even though there are still some dietary limitations on the Revised Simeons' Diet food plan, these new recipes incorporate the approved changes and will spice up your meals and may even spark your own creativity!

There are additional proteins, vegetables and fruits that have been added, so feel free to use your imagination and let this book serve as "the beginning of the end" to the usual boredom of the original Simeons' Diet! Our goal continues to be to encourage everyone who undertakes a weight management program to embrace the transformation and change. Best wishes and bon appétit!

Beth Golden, PhD, ND

SUCCESS STARTS HERE! …
MUST KNOW info

Beth Golden, PhD, ND

Successful weight loss is the goal …
Here is information you need to help you _succeed_!

1. Use a scale to weigh proteins and vegetables at _every_ meal. Weight loss becomes very sensitive to dietary errors.

2. Read the ingredients and nutritional information for _everything_!

3. No fats, starches or sugars: Read **all** ingredient _labels_, not just the "Nutrition Facts". Many ingredient names can be confusing but knowing what to look for not only increases the chance of success with the HCG Diet, but helps you become a better consumer. For example, sugars and sweeteners can be listed by more than 50 different names! These include _fructose, maltodextrin, diastase, dextrose_, etc. (HINT: Maltodextrin can be found in flavored Melba toast and _Crystal Light_.) Soy additives can be found as _hydrolyzed protein_.

4. No oil of any form, other than mineral oil or a light spritz of Pam when grilling may be used. Carefully check all cooking items, body products, and vitamin supplements. Hydrogenated oils, margarine, butter, olive oil or the like are _not_ allowed.

5. Read the ingredients and nutritional information for _everything_!

6. No sugar: Stevia is the preferred sweetener. Aspartame has been reported to have an adverse effect on the hypothalamus gland and may therefore affect short- and/or long-term weight management results. Watch for additives: some brands of powdered Stevia use maltodextrin or other sugars as fillers. Many other sweeteners are chemically based, so it is advisable to eliminate the intake of "sugarless," "diet" or "light" products containing these labels, such as diet drinks, sugarless gum, mints or lozenges.

7. No alcoholic beverages.

8. No dairy except 1 tbsp of milk per day.

9. Read the ingredients and nutritional information for *everything*! (Just making sure this point is not lost!)

10. WATER, WATER, WATER! Drink plenty of pure, mineralized water daily. The daily recommendation is approximately half of your body weight. A good source of pure water is filtered through Reverse Osmosis with added liquid, trace minerals (Concentrated Liquid Ionic Minerals). For days of extra perspiration from exercising or infrared saunas, additional fluids and electrolytes are recommended.

11. WATER IONIZER MACHINES: There are many alkalizing and restructuring water machines on the market, better known as ionizers. We feel they are excellent pieces of equipment and highly recommend them. However, during the HCG Diet, the body is not under the same conditions. We do not recommend drinking alkalized water during the HCG Diet since it creates rapid detox and apparent mineral imbalances. If you do decide to drink water from ionized water machines while on the diet, please seek the advice of a medical professional to monitor your progress and mineral levels.

12. Fruits: Fruits should be consumed at least 3 hours apart. (Tomatoes are actually a fruit but counted as a vegetable on the Simeons' Diet.)

13. Protein portions must be exact: Weight all protein serving. Do not guess. The daily allotted amount of protein is 3 ounces

cooked or 3.5 ounces before cooking twice a day. Free-range is recommended when available and practical because free-range animals are fed grass and, as a result, are leaner. Buffalo meat is an acceptable protein choice and is very lean as a result of being grass fed. Also, Buffalo have NOT been subjected to growth hormones in the way that other meat-producing animals have been.

14. <u>Vegetables can be mixed</u> and a serving of 4 – 6 ounces twice a day is the ideal amount. (up to 6 oz when eating water dense foods)

15. <u>Seasonings:</u> Single seasonings are preferred. Blended seasonings tend to contain at least one non-approved ingredient such as oil or sugar. So, be sure to check labels for non-approved ingredients.

16. <u>Avoid pre-packaged foods:</u> Most pre-packaged foods, such as sliced meats, contain additives and sugar. Check all labels carefully for a complete list of ingredients. As long as you prepare your foods from the actual food, additives are generally not a problem.

17. <u>Chew Food Well:</u> The first stage of good digestion and proper assimilation of food starts in the mouth. By chewing food really well, it not only brings out the flavor better, but provides the opportunity for the enzyme amylase to help properly break down food before delivery into the stomach.

Beth Golden, PhD, ND

TIPS to know BEFORE you begin The HCG Diet

Beth Golden, PhD, ND

HELP! . . . I have to EAT OUT!

Eating out is part of most everyone's life and participating in the HCG Diet doesn't mean you have to miss out on those experiences. Whether it's lunch with co-workers, a birthday dinner for a family member or traveling that keeps you from preparing your own meal(s), here are tips to help keep you on track:

RESTAURANTS: Eating out in a restaurant can still be a pleasurable experience. When it comes to ordering a drink, ask for unsweetened herbal tea, lemon water or black coffee. For your meal, order grilled chicken breast or lean steak; steamed vegetables and/or a side salad, with dressing on the side. Or for dressing, ask for balsamic vinegar or squeeze a bit of fresh lemon on it. When your food arrives, eat only what is allowed on the HCG Diet (no dressing!) and about ½ of the protein (most restaurants serve approximately 6 ounces of protein per meal). You can have a bite or two of a roll (no butter) as your 'starch'. If you don't make a big deal about it . . . no one will know! One of the things you may start noticing, is how much fattening sauce and 'extras' are part of almost every dish prepared in restaurants.

FAST FOOD: Eating at fast food restaurants is generally not recommended, however, in a pinch, most offer various garden salads with grilled chicken. Generally, the salad can be ordered without cheese and without sauces on the chicken. Order an Asian salad with grilled chicken and mandarin oranges or another type of grilled chicken salad, ensuring the chicken is without sauce. Skip the edamame (soy) beans, croutons, dressing, nuts and extras. These general guidelines can be followed at any fast food restaurant.

DELI: Another alternative to hectic schedules and for people *on-the-go* is the grocery store deli. Turkey and chicken breast are readily available at all delis. Confirm that the turkey or chicken breast, or lean beef does not contain sugar, starch or other off-limit ingredients. Since deli meats are sliced and sold by weight, ask them to package your order in 3 ounce servings. Grab an apple on the way out. . . Nothing could be easier!

What's BODY LOTION got to do with it?

Plenty! And here's why ...

The HCG Diet is a **fat-free, oil-free** plan. This includes absorbable oils used on the face or body. Pay *special attention* to face and body products as some contain absorbable oils such as jojoba, sesame and vitamin E, for example. Another hidden culprit can be oils in make-up and sometimes creams for pain.

A lot of people see the word 'oil' in essential oils and misinterpret them as oil that can't be used on the HCG Diet; however, they are perfectly fine. Essential oils are highly concentrated ingredients from nature and are not and 'oil' that absorbs into the body. Be aware that many essential oils are not meant to use directly on the body and are designed to mix with what is called carrier oil, which is usually almond oil. An oil of that nature is definitely not allowed. Also, essential oils are therapeutic to some extent which can affect detoxification, digestion, hormonal levels, and other functions, so know what oils are designed to do before using.

Also, watch *toxic chemicals* and *preservatives* in body products such as parabens, propylene glycol, sodium lauryl sulfate, ammonium lauryl sulfate, and PEG, among others. Many ingredients included in skin care products are considered to be unhealthy and quite toxic.

Beware of "HCG Diet Approved" products. Read labels carefully and make sure they are and make sure they aren't cheap OTC products laden with many of the toxic chemicals as mentioned above.

Golden Essence® makes the <u>only</u> healthy, pure skin care line approved for use during the HCG Diet. These natural products are oil-free, paraben-free, synthetic fragrance-free and synergistically formulated to help nourish and naturally moisturize the face and body.

Made from the highest quality ingredients, *Golden Essence's®* purity works in concert with the dietary restrictions of the HCG Diet. HCG Dieter find they like them so well, they often continue to use them long after the HCG Diet.

You can find all our products listed and approved on the Campaign for Safe Cosmetics website!

For more information, visit:
HCGDietSkincare.com
HCGDietPlan.com

GRISSINI Bread Sticks... *there IS a Difference!*

Before the HCG Diet re-surfaced in 2007, hardly ANYONE had heard of a Grissini, as far as we knew. But as soon as the Simeons' Diet appeared again, we found ourselves wandering down the aisles at the grocery stores looking for 'something' called Grissini. Low and behold, there it was….sure enough….a cardboard box sitting on the top shelf with a picture on the outside of the box with a long "bread stick-looking picture" and, by Joe, it said: **Grissini.** It was almost beyond belief for those of us who have raised families and shopped in grocery stores for YEARS that we never ran across "Grissini". Upon further investigation though, Grissini were thought to have originated in Italy in the 14th Century, however local tradition gives credit to a baker located in Lanzo Torinese (Northern Italy) in 1679. Regardless how they were discovered, they have been around for a LONG time, offered in restaurants and are delicious! In case you are still wondering, the word "grissini" means "thin crisp breadsticks". Grissino is ONE and Grissini are MORE THAN ONE.

Recently, a family owned local bread company located just across the Bay from us in Tampa, Fl named Discovery Foods of America, contacted us to inquire about the HCG Diet. They found out we specialize in the HCG Diet and since they specialize in quality bread products, including Grissini, they wanted to know more about the HCG Diet and how their home-made Grissini might help HCG Dieters! After we explained the oil-free HCG Diet concept to them, one of their owners and 'Grissini EXPERT', Chef Franco, decided to check out Grissini in grocery stores and evaluate calorie and oil content. He felt they are higher in oil, fat and calories than the boxes claim and may be the answer to why we have seen many women who cannot lose as much weight otherwise if they eat the

starch on the on the HCG Diet. So, Chef Franco put on his creative hat and was determined to make a tasty, oil free Grissini for HCG dieters!

After several attempts and my entire staff tasting lots of Grissini for a couple of weeks from his kitchen, Chef Franco hit the mark and created a winner! His new and improved, oil-free Grissini are out of this world! Based on his other recipes, I asked him if he could make them in varying flavors, which he has. His Grissini come in rosemary and sage, and whole wheat. Best of all, we are happy to report that the research we conducted in our HCG Diet Clinics has proven that Chef Franco's oil-free Grissini now give the HCG Dieter the ability to eat Grissini more often than before and not compromise any weight loss! In addition to the new found success with these oil-free Grissini and HCG Dieters, we also like that Discover Foods of America operates a FDA approved manufacturing facility with American ingredients made by Americans. Their products rate high on our list because of this; along with the fact their products are preservative-free and other additive-free products.

TIPS for adding Chef Franco's Oil-Free Grissini to your HCG Diet:
- Crush Grissini for a flavorful coating on zucchini, sliced onions or other select vegetables before baking in the oven
- Break up Grissini into small pieces and use as croutons in soup or on top salads
- Breadsticks in various flavors go well with fish
- Try wrapping breadsticks in slices of turkey breast and a thin slice of cucumber for a spectacular appetizer

SPICE up your DIET … and your LIFE!

Cooking with all sorts of SPICES livens up the flavor of food and the list of the ones that are allowed on the HCG Diet is almost endless. There is no limit to the creativity that can be had through the use of spices on proteins and vegetables. Use caution, however. Double check pre-blended spices and be sure to read all labels! Sugar-free and fat-free are just words. Stay away from any added ingredients such as: hydrolyzed protein, soy protein, fructose, glucose, dextrose and maltodextrin, just to name a few. Make sure your spices just contain spices!

Here is a list of suggested spices and add-ins that can be combined to make a variety of seasonings and flavors. Feel free to omit or add to these. And be sure to check out the *Seasonings* section for creative ideas for blending these spices together.

Allspice	Mace
Apple cider vinegar	Nutmeg
Basil	Old Bay Seasoning
Bragg Liquid Aminos	Onion powder
Cardamom	Oregano
Celery powder	Paprika
Chili powder	Parsley
Cilantro	Pepper / Peppercorns
Cinnamon	Poultry seasoning
Cloves	Pure cocoa powder (sparingly)
Coriander	Rosemary
Cumin	Sage
Dill	Sea salt
Dry mustard	Thyme
Garlic / garlic powder	Turmeric
Ginger	White vinegar

SPICES cont.

With limitation, the following may be used, as well:

Hot sauce: ensure that it is sugar-alcohol- and/or jalapeno-free; and use sparingly.

Lemon or Lime juice: limited to the total combined juice of 1 per day.

COOKING TIPS: Handy Hints for the KITCHEN

BROTH:

Beef and chicken broth are great for cooking but, as of this writing, all store-bought broths contain one or more ingredients not approved for use with the HCG Diet. Looking at the ingredients, you will find sugar, honey, dextrose, MSG, partially hydrolyzed cotton seed oil, carrots, green pepper, hydrolyzed wheat gluten and more. Therefore, until a sugar-free, fat-free broth is made, it is recommended that you only use the broths found in this cookbook. *See* p. 161-163. *Never* use reconstituted bouillon cubes.

CAULIFLOWER:

1. When buying fresh cauliflower, look for white or cream-colored heads that are firm and free of dark spots or other blemishes.
2. Store it unwashed in a perforated or open plastic bag in the refrigerator for up to one week; wash just before preparing.
3. Steam or boil and serve as a side dish seasoned with tarragon or nutmeg. (After the Diet, sprinkle with Parmesan cheese!)
4. Break cauliflower into flowerets and roast in the oven with onions and garlic; add to vegetable or chicken broth with other vegetables for a healthful soup. Puree for a creamy texture.
5. Mock mashed potatoes: Cook until very tender, mash, then season with sea salt and pepper for a delicious alternative to mashed potatoes. For garlic mashed potatoes, add 1-2 cloves of minced garlic per pound of cauliflower before cooking. (After the Diet, add a little organic butter!) 1 serving = 4 oz.

CHICKEN/TURKEY BREAST:

1. When pan-searing/cooking chicken breasts, flatten meat with mallet to approximately 1/2" thick then pierce with fork; sprinkle with seasonings then cook.
2. Use medium-high heat to cook chicken breasts. Avoid cooking over LOW or medium heat because the juices will be drawn to the surface before the chicken browns.
3. To reduce the loss of juices from chicken breasts, use tongs instead of a fork to turn.
4. Marinate chicken to add flavor and make chicken juicier. Make a mixture of your favorite seasonings, pierce chicken with fork, sprinkle with seasonings and marinate in refrigerator for 1 to 2 hours.
5. Poaching: Heat water or chicken broth to boiling. Add chicken breasts to pan in a single layer; reduce heat to LOW. Cover and simmer about 20 minutes or until juice of chicken is clear when centers of thickest pieces are cut.
6. Test doneness with a meat thermometer. For a whole chicken, insert an ovenproof thermometer so the tip is in the thickest part of the inside thigh and doesn't touch the bone. Roast until thermometer reads 165° F and juice of chicken is clear when center of thigh is cut.
7. To preserve the juices of the chicken, cook quickly in a skillet and test for doneness only as often as necessary.
8. Brine chicken in sea salt, water and spices before cooking. (Suggested spices: chopped garlic and thyme, 1 tsp rosemary, 1 tsp sage) Submerge in brine in refrigerator: chicken breasts pieces - 1 to 2 hours; whole chicken - 8 to 12 hours. OR dilute 1 cup Bragg Liquid Aminos with 3 cups water and add ¼ cup chopped garlic and ¼ cup ginger.

COFFEE:

Don't waste that extra coffee! Place remaining coffee (or, if brewing fresh, coffee cooled to room temperature) in a blender and add ice. Add Stevia to taste. Blend to desired consistency and serve. For an extra touch of flavor, add a pinch of cinnamon, pure cocoa powder or other flavorful spices before blending.

CROCK POT COOKING:

1. Place a large amount of lean beef in a crock pot and cook on LOW for 4-8 hours with 2-4 cups of water or herb tea. Before cooking, season with herbs and spices, as desired. Add onion, mushrooms, and celery for flavor. This makes the most tender and moist meats. When done and cooled, weigh into 3 oz portions and freeze anything that you won't use within 3 days.
2. Use leftover broth to make savory soups. Just add the daily portion of vegetables, like asparagus, cabbage or spinach, to 1 cup of the broth. If more liquid is preferred, add herb tea or water and season.

FISH:

Fish is done when the meat is no longer transparent and flakes easily with a fork.

You may prefer to grill fish outdoors to avoid fish odors from permeating your house. If so, be sure to use the top rack on the grill to avoid over-cooking. Also, use tin foil with a little water *or* cook on parchment paper (in oven only).

LEMONS:

Slice a whole lemon into wedges and keep in refrigerator in air tight container or zip Lock bag.

(Total juice of 1 lemon is allowed per day). If not in season, then reconstituted lemon juice is perfect and easy to use. Substitution amounts are listed on bottle label.

MEATS:

When cooking meat or fish, season the pan with sea salt, pepper (if desired) and herbs before placing meat or fish in pan. This helps prevent sticking. Add a few tablespoons of water or herb tea for added moisture to the meat.

MUSHROOMS:

To clean: Peel off outer layer of mushroom skin starting on the underneath side. Place blade of a sharp knife perpendicular to underneath edge where skin begins and hold between knife and finger. As you begin to pull skin (like peeling a banana), turn mushroom right side up and skin will peel off all the way to the top center of the mushroom. Slice off any remaining outside skin with knife. Discard all peel. If stem is spongy, remove and discard. (This should remove most dirt. If not, quickly rinse in water, but do not submerge or the mushrooms will soak up water and get soggy).

PARCHMENT PAPER:

Parchment paper is great for cooking in the oven as it will not burn; it keeps meats from sticking to the pan and allows for baking or broiling without the use of oil or butter.

SPICES AND SEASONINGS:

Every effort was made to ensure that the amount of seasonings and spices for each recipe *enhances* the flavor of the vegetable, fruit or protein being prepared. However, feel free to increase or decrease recommended amounts to suit your taste.

The SKINNY on STEVIA ... and other sweeteners

Stevia is a calorie-free, sugar-free sweetener made from the Stevia plant and is the sweetener of choice for the HCG Diet.

Stevia is found in many of the following recipes. Unless otherwise indicated, *powdered* Stevia is the type of Stevia used. Liquid Stevia may also be used, generally only 1 or 2 drops at a time.

IMPORTANT: Plain powdered Stevia is now available in all health food stores and most grocery stores. However, read the ingredients of pre-packaged Stevia, as some contain *added sugar* or non-approved sugar substitutes or fillers. Alternatively, pure powdered Stevia can be purchased from bulk-herb retailers.

Flavored Stevia is available online and also in health food stores; available brands include Sweetleaf® and Stevita®. Flavors can be found in vanilla, root beer, chocolate and more and can be used with coffee, tea and more. *See* Beverages on p. 70 and Blender Bursts on p. 77.

DRINKS WITH STEVIA: Some beverages advertising the use of Stevia contain additional sugar. Zevia® brand drinks contain Stevia but also have 13 grams of carbohydrates from other sugar ingredients. Read the ingredients!

DRINKS WITH ARTIFICIAL SWEETENERS: Hansen's® Diet drinks and Diet Rite® have been found to include only Splenda® and no other sugary sweeteners; both are zero calorie, zero carbohydrate beverages.

Beth Golden, PhD, ND

I have a FAMILY (and a LIFE) … How can I do THIS?

Because we all have diverse work and family schedules, we often have little time to prepare meals. Here are some time saving tips for success.

1. Buy and prepare each week's worth of HCG Diet foods all at once.

2. Pick a day out of the week to prepare and have your family, especially the kids, help with the preparation. This frees up a lot of time and is easy as 1-2-3.

3. Buy fruit for the week. Pre-wash and leave them accessible for the entire family to enjoy! Pre-cut and section oranges and grapefruit; place in ready-to-go bags or containers.

4. Buy vegetables for the week. Lettuce, spinach, broccoli, tomatoes, onions, cucumbers and asparagus, just to name a few. Slice or chop each and place portions into zip Lock bags or airtight containers…ready to eat, toss in a salad or cook with. You can even precook the vegetables and then bag them.

5. Buy and portion a week's worth of meats: chicken or turkey breast, veal, fish, and steak. Cut and store in 3 ½ oz portions. You can also ask the butcher to pre-cut your selections into 3 ½ oz portions. Another great suggestion is to have the butcher ground fresh turkey breast, chicken breast, veal and/or lean steak so you'll have the correct fat-free proteins.

6. Pre-bake 3-4 chicken breasts in foil or parchment paper with lemon juice, ½ tsp thyme, ½ tsp garlic powder and ¼ tsp

rosemary. Do the same for fish or veal. When done, weigh and bag individual 3 oz portions and freeze ½ of the meat for the 2nd half of the week. Choose Eat 2 different meats daily. This way they are ready to grab and go for work, to toss into a recipe or salad, or quickly heat in the microwave with vegetables.

7. Make herb teas and lemonade (*see* p. 75) by the gallon. This way you always have something refreshing to drink. Sweeten teas with Stevia: powdered, liquid or flavored to taste.

MORE TIPS, TRICKS and TIDBITS

1. Each day you take HCG, Dr. Simeons estimated the body releases 2,000 calories of stored fat. Research indicates that if more food than recommended is consumed, the body stops the process of weight and fat loss.

2. Great teas to help satisfy the need for flavor are: mint tea, spearmint tea, orange tea, raspberry tea, spiced teas, vanilla tea or any lively flavored teas.

3. Keep a quart or half-gallon of Stevia-sweetened lemonade or herbal tea in the refrigerator to quench thirst and ward off sweet cravings. (*See* recipe for Lemonade, p. 73).

4. Enjoy Wisdom of the Ancients brand Yerba Matte Royale Instant Tea. The natural caffeine and nutrients can boost energy, purify the body, increase metabolism and suppress the appetite. Yerba Matte also contains vitamins, minerals and chlorophyll. There are tribal people in the Indies who actually live on this beneficial herb. It is very nutritious and is great for breakfast, in between meals or with a meal.

5. Create a coffee and tea bar in the kitchen....keep calorie-free sweeteners out and use them freely as flavorings for drinks and cooking.

6. Table salt is high in sodium and increases water retention. However, natural sea salt contains beneficial nutrients and does not create this reaction. Depression has actually been linked to sodium deficiency but not the sodium found in table salt. So, to increase natural sodium, use only sea salt.

7. When in the grocery store, shop the perimeter of the store – this is where the freshest and healthiest food, i.e. fruits, vegetables, meats, fish, can be found.

8. ORGANIC BEEF is lower in fat because it is grass fed rather than grain and/or corn fed and has no growth hormones. Whether buying filet mignon, prime rib, sirloin or another selection of beef, always choose the highest grade with little to no visible fat to ensure the leanest beef.

WILD CAUGHT vs. FARM RAISED FISH: To benefit fully from participation in the HCG Diet, wild-caught fish should be selected over farm-raised when available and practical.

The *REVISED* Simeons' HCG Diet

Beth Golden, PhD, ND

The Revised Simeons' HCG Diet

- Eat only foods listed – Eat any time of day
- No oils of any form, including body lotion.
  EXCEPTION: mineral oil is acceptable**
- Drink at least 8 - 10 cups of pure, mineralized water daily
- Weigh all protein

Upon Rising: (Optional) 1-2 glasses of lemon water (warm or cold)
– may sweeten with Stevia, if desired

Breakfast: Unlimited amounts of any or all of the following
throughout the day:

- Organic Regular or Decaf coffee; Lipton-type tea in any quantity (watch for too much caffeine if drinking coffee and caffeinated tea);
- Any organic herbal teas, such as: Yerba Matte; Green tea; Oolong tea, Chamomile, or flavored teas;
- Soda Water, Mineral Water, Spring Water, Sparkling Water;
- **No Alkaline Water** during Diet: creates TOO much rapid detox and mineral imbalances.

Lunch:

1. **Protein Foods: 3 ½ oz RAW or 3 oz COOKED**
   - Choose one <u>lean</u> protein: Pages 31, 37, 87
     1. Lean Veal or Lean Steak (free-range recommended)
     2. Fresh White Fish: Crab, Flounder, Halibut, Lobster, Haddock, Cod, Sole, Shrimp, Stone Crab, Tilapia, Swordfish, Bass, Pike, Brooke Trout, Jew Fish, John Dory or Snapper.
     3. Chicken Breast or Turkey Breast – white meat - no skin
     4. Maximum 2 times a month: 3 egg whites + 1 whole egg
   - Remove all visible fat. Steam, broil or grill without additional fat.
   - **NO:** hamburger, pork, salmon, eel, tuna, herring, DRIED, PICKLED or SMOKED fish, Chilean sea bass or fatty fish.

2. Fresh Vegetables: 4 – 6 oz SERVING of any of the following or any combination:

- Asparagus, Beet Greens, Broccoli, Brussels Sprouts, Cabbage, Cauliflower, Celery, Chard, Chicory, Cucumbers, Endive, Fennel, Green Salad, Green Beans, Kale, Lettuce, Mushrooms, Onions, Red Radishes, Soy Sprouts, Spinach, Tomatoes and Zucchini.

NO other vegetables – **NO** potato, sweet potato, carrots, corn, lima beans, soy beans, legumes, green peas, rice, eggplant, palm heart, artichoke, any type of bell pepper or avocado.

3. Starch (optional)

- One breadstick (grissino/grissini); one plain Melba toast; *or* fat free, sugar free pretzels. (about 30 calories total)

Mid-Day Fruit: Choose One

- Apple, Orange, handful of Strawberries, ½ Grapefruit, 2 Kiwis **NO** other types of fruits

Dinner: Same 3 Categories as Lunch

Evening Fruit: Choose One:

- Apple, Orange, handful of Strawberries, ½ Grapefruit, 2 Kiwis **NO** other types of fruits

Allowed:

- Juice of 1 Lemon or Lime daily (combined total. Equivalent conversion available on reconstituted bottled juice);
- One tablespoon of Skim Milk daily (optional);
- Sweetener: Stevia is preferred. Saccharin and Splenda® contain maltodextrin - 4 calories per gram;
- Sea Salt, Pepper, Vinegar, Mustard Powder, Garlic (1/2 – 1 clove), Sweet-Basil, Parsley, Thyme, Marjoram, and other leaf spices are freely available as seasonings;
- ** Salad Dressing: 1 tbsp. Mineral Oil, Garlic and Seasonings;

- 1 - 3 small cups of diet soda (no aspartame) allowed daily – Diet Rite and Hansen's are sweetened with Splenda®. Some people lose MORE weight when they DO NOT drink any diet soda. Herbal teas or lemon mixed with sparkling water can be a nice treat too!

Not Allowed

- NO Margarine, Butter, Oil, or Dressings
- NO Rice or Pasta
- NO Sugar, Fructose, Aspartame (Equal), or other type of Sweetener.

Beth Golden, PhD, ND

SHOPPING LIST
For The *REVISED* Simeons' HCG Diet

Beth Golden, PhD, ND

SHOPPING LIST For The <u>REVISED</u> Simeons' HCG Diet
Purchase items a few days before you are ready to begin

PROTEIN (Beef/Poultry/Fish)
Boneless Skinless Chicken Breast
Boneless Skinless Turkey Breast
Lean Grass Fed Beef or Organic
Lean Grass Fed Veal
White Fish (Crab, Flounder, Halibut,
   Lobster, Haddock, Cod, Sole,
   Shrimp, Stone Crab, Tilapia,
   Swordfish, Bass, Pike, Brooke Trout,
   Jew Fish, John Dory or Snapper)

FRUITS
Grapefruit
Apples
Strawberries
Kiwi
Oranges
Lemons
Reconstituted Lemon Juice
Limes

VEGETABLES

Broccoli
Cucumbers
Cabbages
Celery
All Onions
Garlic
Spinach
Brussels sprouts
Endive
Mushrooms
All types of Lettuce
Green Beans

Soy Sprouts
Tomatoes
Beet Greens (tops only)
Asparagus
Chard
Radishes
Chicory
Cauliflower
Fennel
Zucchini (No squash)
Kale

BEVERAGES/CONDIMENTS/OTHER

Natural Teas
Sea Salt
Diet Soda (no Aspartame)
Water
Mineral Water
Melba Toast / Hard Pretzels
Bragg Liquid Aminos

Organic Decaf or Regular Coffee
Leaf Spices
Herbs
Stevia (preferred sweetener)
Milk
Grissino/Grissini (Bread Sticks)
Vinegar: Bragg Apple Cider
Balsamic, Wine or Rice:
   stop if weight stalls*
*see Research Section on p. 184-85

Use an Accurate Food Scale

I'm done with the Diet…
NOW WHAT?

Beth Golden, PhD, ND

The 21-Day Transition Phase
Add all foods *EXCEPT* sugar and starch

Stop taking the HCG and continue the Diet for 72 more hours. At the end of the 72 hours, you can eat anything you please, *except* sugar and starch, provided you faithfully observe one simple rule: **weigh every morning** (without clothes) *after* you get out of bed and empty your bladder and *before* breakfast or liquids of any kind. It is important that you keep a portable bathroom scale at hand, particularly while traveling.

It takes about 3 weeks (21 days) before the weight reached at the end of the diet becomes stable, meaning it does not show violent fluctuations after an occasional excess. During this 21-day period, carbohydrates, such as sugar, rice, bread, corn, potatoes, pastries, etc, are by far the most dangerous. When these carbohydrates are **NOT CONSUMED**, fats can be introduced somewhat more liberally. A small glass of wine with meals may be introduced once a week, if desired, as long as weight stays stable. However we recommend NO ALCHOHOL at this time. Discontinue if you cannot stabilize your weight.

This has to be observed very carefully during the first 3 weeks (21 days) after the diet has ended, otherwise, weight gain is very likely. As soon as fats and starches (sugars) are **combined**, weight gain can get out of hand.

Skipping a meal
As long as your weight stays within 2 pounds (over or below) of the weight reached after the 72 hours at the end of the diet, continue to eat as you have been. However, if weight *increases* beyond two pounds, even if only by a few ounces, enjoy what is called a "steak

day". Dr. Simeons was brilliant in his discovery of weight management and his "steak day" protocol still works today!

Skip breakfast and lunch and drink plenty of non-calorie liquids throughout the day (i.e.: herbal teas, water, etc.). At dinner, eat a grass fed, organic steak (size/fat content does not matter) and 1 apple *OR* 1 raw tomato – nothing else. Simeons discovered it was of the utmost importance that this was done on the day the scale went above 2 pounds and not postponed until the following day. It has been shown that if the daytime meals are skipped on the day in which a gain is registered in the morning, an immediate drop of a pound or more should result. But if skipping breakfast and lunch, not just having a light meal, is postponed, the phenomenon does not occur and several days of strict dieting may be necessary to correct the situation. The extra weight will be stored as fat.

Dr. Simeons said: "You should hardly ever need to skip a meal. If you have eaten a heavy breakfast or lunch, you may feel no desire to eat dinner, and in this case no increase in weight takes place. If you keep your weight the same as it was on the last day at the end of the Diet, even a heavy dinner does not usually cause an increase of the mentioned two pounds and will not require any special eating alterations."

Dr. Simeons also reported that people were surprised how small their appetite had become and what they could eat without gaining weight. He found that many no longer suffered from an abnormal appetite and they also felt satisfied with less food.

Losing more weight
Dr. Simeons also told people: ". . . you ***should not lose more than 2 pounds*** either because the loss will be at the expense of normal

fat. Any normal fat that is loss is invariably regained as soon as more food is taken and it usually results in a greater than 2 pound gain." If your weight decreases more than 2 lbs, gradually increase your food intake to get back within 2 lbs of your final weight.

Beware of Over-enthusiasm

After the diet has ended, Dr. Simeons found that some people were skeptical that they could resume eating normally. He warned people not to continue to diet after they finished the hCG Diet by only adding a few things to the 500 calorie diet or they would gain weight. A good rule of thumb is to eat at least 4 – 5 times a day. To *maintain muscle*, divide your body weight by 10 and eat at least that many ounces of protein daily. To *build muscle*, eat at least 50% more.

Relapses

Dr. Simeons had 60% to 70% of his cases who experienced little or no difficulty in permanently holding their weight. Dr. Simeons said when relapses did occur it was usually due to negligence in the basic rule of daily weighing. Many people think daily weighing is not necessary, but that is based on guidelines from other weight loss programs that advocate weighing only once a week. That may be true for their programs, however, after the HCG diet most people find they cannot judge an increase or decrease in weight from the way their body feels and the way their clothes fit. One of the biggest mistakes people make is to not carry a scale while traveling. This is a disastrous mistake because after a course on this plan, as much as 10 lbs can be regained without any noticeable change since newly acquired fat is first evenly distributed and does not show the former preference for certain body parts.

Women who do the HCG diet during the year *after* the last menstruation (at the onset of menopause) do just as well as others, but Simeons reported a higher relapse rate until such time that menopause is fully established. This is attributed to the hormonal imbalances experienced during menopause.

Should you experience weight gain or want to lose additional weight, participating in an additional short 21-day course of HCG and the Diet is completely acceptable. Repeat courses are often even more satisfactory than the first time and you have the advantage of knowing how you will feel on the plan.

Saliva tests to evaluate hormone levels such as cortisol, DHEA, etc are extremely beneficial. Visit our website for more information.

SHOPPING LIST

for the 21-DAY TRANSITION PHASE

SHOPPING LIST for the 21-DAY TRANSITION PHASE

Grass fed beef, fish from the ocean and organic foods are recommended when possible.

PROTEIN (no restrictions)
Beef
Pork
Veal
Poultry
Fish
Dairy (cheese, cottage cheese, yogurt)
Eggs
Butter (not margarine), as noted in #1 on next page

VEGETABLES
All, except as noted in #2 on next page

FRUITS
All, except as noted in #3 on next page

BEVERAGES/CONDIMENTS
All, except those containing sugars or starch
All sugar free (avoid alcohol)

NUTS
All, except peanuts (peanuts are not really nuts, they are legumes).
Restrict amount to 7-10 nuts 1 to 2 times a day.

IMPORTANT TIPS TO FOLLOW WHILE IN THE 21-DAY TRANSITION:

1) Add fats back into your diet in moderation (organic butter, oils, Flax, Omega oils, coconut oil). Avoid trans fats such as hydrogenated or partially hydrogenated oils.

2) Limit daily amounts of peas, carrots and beets. Avoid corn.

3) Passion fruits should be avoided during this phase. Limit fruit to 1 a day.

4) Remember, **NO** starches or sugars are allowed during this phase. Sugars include, but are not limited to: sugar, corn syrup, fructose, high fructose, molasses, and maltodextrin. Starches include, but are not limited to: CORN, potatoes, beans, soy products (including soy sauce), tofu, breads, rice, crackers, flour products, oats, pastas, pretzels, sprouted grains, cookies and cakes.

THE 21-DAY STABILIZATION PHASE
Add all foods back into the diet

This is an *extremely important* part of the plan and an exciting phase, because it begins to incorporate all of the food groups back into your diet. Only because this is unchartered territory after weight loss and people commonly are concerned about gaining weight, some people feel more comfortable with planning their food each day until they know their limits. This tends to produce the best results.

However, others begin enjoying the freedom of being able to eat whatever they want within moderation. Dr. Simeons felt (and we do too) it's best to allow you to eat as you please; focus on healthy guidelines; and enjoy the freedom from dietary restrictions and learn how much food your body does or does not need . . . At this point you can:

- Begin to add all food categories;
- Include (in small servings) beans, whole grain breads, potatoes, brown rice, whole wheat crackers, whole grain flour products, oats, pastas, pretzels, sprouted grains, etc.;
- Include all fruits, vegetables, meats, fish or starches. Some people find some fruits (papaya, mangos, bananas, etc.) and alcohol contains too many carbohydrates and cause weight gain. But the general rule is that you can begin to eat most anything you please. Remember, weigh every single day without fail!

Weigh *EVERY* morning after voiding (without fail)

SUGGESTED GUIDELINES

- Eat organic food
- Eat at least 5 times a day –*always* eat breakfast
- Consume at least 15 – 20 ounces of protein a day (adjust according to individual weight)
- Minimum daily ounces of protein: divide body weight by 10. Daily fat grams: 30 – 50 grams of fat
- Daily caloric intake should be approx. 1500 – 2500 calories (adjust according to individual weight)
- Eat 1-2 fruits (preferably organic) per day if weight stays stable; reduce if needed
- Drink half of your body weight in pure water
- Support the digestive process
- Reduce stress and support nervous system
- Ensure high doses of pro-biotics for good flora levels
- Get regular exercise
- Do Infrared sauna sessions at least 3 – 4 times a week

As the body is re-adjusting during these 21 days, weight can fluctuate. Most people find that sticking to the above guidelines offers the best results. However, if your weight ***increases*** over 2 pounds, drink liquids the entire day (herbal teas; non-caloric drinks, etc.). For dinner, the protocol is to eat a large steak (preferably grass-fed, organic) and 1 apple, tomato or mixed green salad (apple cider vinegar dressing is OK).

If weight ***decreases*** more than 2 pounds, increase intake of food gradually to maintain a weight within 2 lbs of end weight.

DO NOT stay on a low calorie diet as *the body will begin to store fat!* And **AVOID** (when possible) corn, white sugar, corn syrup, fructose, high fructose, molasses, maltodextrin, white flour, trans fats, such as hydrogenated or partially hydrogenated "anything" and aspartame (research indicates it has a negative effect on the hypothalamus – among other things)

Most people have stabilized their weight by now, but occasionally some may find that it still takes time for their weight reached at the end of the HCG Diet to become stable. People who cannot stabilize their weight after several months are generally consuming too much alcohol (sugar), too many carbohydrates (converts to sugar) and/or they have food sensitivities and should be tested and eliminate offending foods.

As soon as fats and starch are **_combined_**, weight gain can get out of hand. This has to be observed very carefully during these 3 weeks or weight gain and abnormal fat is very likely.

Dr. Golden has formulated a product called Sta-Lean that specifically addresses the body's needs AFTER the HCG Diet. You can find it on the HCGDietPlan.com website or purchase from one of our retail locations.

Skipping a meal - At your morning weigh in, should your weight exceed 2 lbs of the weight reached at the end of the diet, the protocol is to have a "steak day." This involves consuming nothing but calorie-free liquids, such as water and herbal tea, throughout the day and, at dinner time, enjoying a steak (size does not matter) and 1 apple *OR* 1 raw tomato - nothing else. For additional information on the "steak day", please refer back to the 21-day Transition - *Skipping a meal*, p. 43.

Gaining and Losing more weight - It is imperative that the corrective "steak day" be done the same day as discovering your weight has exceeded the allotted 2 lb fluctuation. It is also just as important to gradually increase your food intake if your weight drops below the 2 lb fluctuation. Any normal fat that is loss is invariably regained as soon as more food is taken, and it usually results in a greater than 2 pound gain.

Relapses - As explained in the first transition details, Dr. Simeons had 60% to 70% of his cases who experienced little or no difficulty in maintaining their successful weight and fat loss. Daily weighing remains critical as most people cannot judge an increase or decrease in weight from the way the body feels and the way clothes fit. If traveling, a portable scale is a necessity. Not weighing daily can prove to be disastrous to long-term success. As much as 10 lbs can be regained without any noticeable change since newly acquired fat is first evenly distributed and does not show the former preference for certain body parts.

If you have recently gone through, or are currently going through, menopause, please refer back to the prior transition material for Simeons' findings and observations on menopause-related relapse. Should you experience weight gain or want to lose additional weight, participating in an additional short 21-day course of HCG and the Diet is completely acceptable. Repeat courses are often even more satisfactory than the first time and you have the advantage of knowing how you will feel on the plan.

SPECIAL RECIPE CONTRIBUTIONS
by CHEF CHOUINARD

SPECIAL RECIPE CONTRIBUTIONS

by

CHEF CHOUINARD

Chef Joseph Chouinard is no newcomer to creating exquisite dishes with some of the most rigid restrictions. He and his family have over 80 years of combined experience in the restaurant and catering industry and he has personally overcome some of the strictest catering requests from famous Hollywood stars, as well as in his own personal catering business.

Chef Chouinard's career has taken him to many exquisite and award-winning restaurants including **Anthony's Pier 4**, Boston, MA; **Windows on the World** and **Le Cirque**, New York, NY; **Nikolai's Roof**, Atlanta, GA; **Chouinard's of Charleston**, Charleston, SC; **The Redwoods** and **Pacific Wave**, St. Petersburg, FL; and **F & B Catering** in LOWs Angeles, CA. In 2009, he took his expertise back to Florida where he opened **Chouinard's Cuisine On the Run**, a full service event/planning catering company and café.

His education includes being a graduate from the Culinary Institute of America, as well as an apprenticeship at the 5-star **La Vieille Maison** restaurant. He also attended Florida International University with a focus on hotel restaurant management.

We have the distinguished honor of having Chef Chouinard create tantalizing recipes specifically for the HCG Diet. His initial contributions were overwhelmingly approved by a select group of HCG Dieters. He promises to continue to create and share recipes for the HCG Diet and looks forward to working with the research and development of more HCG Diet recipes.

Chef Chouinard says, "I have been blessed in my career with a wonderfully supportive family and so many great mentors and I look forward to continuing to contribute and create."

We thank him for the following contributions and wish you "Bon appétit!"

Recipes by CHEF CHOUINARD

Tomato Cucumber Salad
(one serving is 4 oz: 1 vegetable)

2 Roma tomatoes, sliced ¼ inch slices
½ peeled cucumber, leaving thin strips of peel in-between:
    slice into ¼ inch slices
⅛ to ¼ red onion, sliced ⅛ inch thick
¼ cup apple cider vinegar
¼ tsp garlic, minced
Stevia, to taste
Sprigs of fresh dill
Pinch sea salt
Pinch coarse ground pepper

In a small bowl, combine cider vinegar, garlic, Stevia and dill. Wisk together. Arrange in a baking dish: sliced tomatoes, cucumbers and onions. Pour vinegar mixture on top and Sprinkle with sea salt. Marinate for one hour. Stack the tomatoes, onions and cucumbers and serve on a chilled plate. Sprinkle with coarse ground pepper.

Poached Chicken Breast with Tomato Basil Coulis
(makes 4 servings: 1 protein, 1 vegetable)

14 oz chicken
14 oz chicken broth (*see* recipes, p. 161 & 162)
14 oz vine ripe tomatoes, diced
2 oz sweet onion, diced
2 tbsp garlic, thinly sliced
4 sprigs basil leaves, chopped
Sea salt, to taste

In a sauce pan, combine tomatoes, garlic and onions. Simmer on LOW heat for 15 minutes. Remove from heat, puree in a blender. Add basil last and pulse for 3 seconds. Add sea salt to taste.

Bring chicken broth to a boil in a pan big enough to hold broth and chicken, place chicken in broth and simmer on LOW for 8-10 minutes. Remove chicken from broth and pour tomato coulis on top and serve.

Bamboo Steamed Scallops with Ginger and Lemon Grass Essence
(makes 4 servings: 1 protein, 1 vegetable)

14 oz fresh scallop's (approx. 16-18 scallops)
½ stalk lemon grass, minced finely
1 small bulb of ginger peeled and finely chopped
1 tbsp garlic finely chopped
½ cup Bragg Liquid Aminos diluted with ½ cup water
Stevia, to taste
4 tops broccoli
8 tops cauliflower
¼ bunch cilantro sprigs

Place lemon grass, ginger and garlic in a bowl with Bragg's. Wisk and add scallops. Marinate for 1 hour.

Place the scallops in a bamboo steamer with broccoli and cauliflower. Place over pot of boiling water and steam for approximately 3 minutes. In the meantime, pour marinade in a pan with Stevia and bring to boil. Remove scallops and veggies from the pan and place onto 4 plates. Strain soy ginger dip on plate of steamed scallops and vegetables. Garnish with cilantro sprigs.

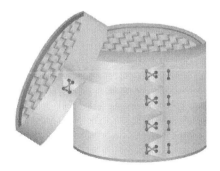

Bamboo Steamer

Beth Golden, PhD, ND

Revised
Simeons' HCG Diet
RECIPES

APPETIZERS

APPETIZERS

Melba Toast Brochette
(makes 1 serving: 1 vegetable, 1 starch)

3 ½ oz tomatoes, diced (cut in ½ first and squeeze out seeds)
½ oz onion, diced
¼ tsp garlic, minced
Cilantro, to taste
1 tsp lemon juice
½ tsp Bragg Apple Cider Vinegar (optional)
2 sprigs fresh basil leaves (optional)
2 sprigs fresh oregano leaves (optional)
Stevia, to taste
Pinch of sea salt
1 plain Melba toast (total 30 calories)

Stir tomatoes, onions, seasonings and lemon juice together. Add optional ingredients, if desired. Add sea salt to taste. Serve on top of Melba toast.

Stuffed Mushrooms (Crab, Lobster or Shrimp)
(makes 1 serving: 1 protein, 1 vegetable, 1 starch, ½ of skim milk)

4 mushrooms (pull out stems)
3 oz cooked crab, Lobster or shrimp, finely chopped
1 ½ oz red onion and celery, finely chopped
1 grissini, finely ground
Pinch of garlic powder
Pinch of sea salt
3 sprigs of dill chopped
1 tsp lemon juice (to moisten mixture)
Dash of water (enough to blend the grissini and spices together)
½ tbsp skim milk

Wash mushrooms & pat dry. Chop seafood and mix with remaining ingredients. Stuff mixture into mushroom caps. Place in baking pan and add water to the pan ¼ way up the mushrooms to steam them as they bake. Bake at 350° covered with foil for 15-20 minutes, or until warm all the way through.

Southwestern Lettuce or Cabbage Wraps
(makes 1 serving: 1 protein, 1 vegetable)

3 ½ oz lean beef, chicken or turkey breast, shrimp or fish

1-2 Romaine leaves *OR* cooked cabbage leaves

2 mushrooms, rinsed and sliced

½ tomato, diced

⅛ onion, sliced

¼ cup water

Spices:
- Pinch of sea salt
- Pinch of pepper
- 3 sprigs cilantro chopped
- Pinch of cumin
- Pinch of coriander
- Pinch of chili powder

For use with beef: cut beef into strips, season to taste with Taco seasoning (*see* recipe, p. 169) and brown in non-stick skillet with a small amount of water. (For others, cook until done all the way through.) Sauté mushrooms, onions and tomatoes in water. Add beef or other protein, spices and then wrap in lettuce or cabbage leaves.

BEVERAGES

Beth Golden, PhD, ND

BEVERAGES

Tip: Any recipe including lemon or lime juice needs to be calculated toward the daily allotment of the juice of 1 lemon!

Kiwi-Lemon Spritzer
(makes 1 serving: 1 fruit)

2 kiwis, peeled
½ tbsp lemon juice
12 oz seltzer water
Stevia, to taste
Ice cubes

Cut kiwi into chunks. Add kiwi and lemon juice to food processor and blend until smooth. Pour mixture through wire mesh strainer into glass of ice. Add seltzer water and Stevia and enjoy!

Sweet n' Sour Lemonade
(makes 2 – 8 oz servings)

16 oz water
1 tbsp lemon juice
Stevia, to taste
Ice cubes

Mix water, lemon juice and Stevia in a pitcher. Add ice as desired.

Serve and enjoy!

Sparkling Delight aka HCG Diet Soda
(makes 1 serving)

8 - 12 oz unflavored sparkling water*
Flavored liquid Stevia of choice**
    (1-3 drops or to taste)
Ice Cubes

Pour sparkling water over ice cubes, add flavored Stevia, to taste and enjoy!

This drink is designed for the soda lover - or for the times when you crave something more than just water. Keep in mind, drinking plain water is still critical to your success and your health. Drink 'Sparkling Delight' in moderation.

*Sparkling water is carbonated water and is the same as soda water, club soda and seltzer water.

**Flavored liquid Stevia is available in many flavors. Sweet Leaf is a recommended brand that makes all-natural flavors such as

Root Beer	Chocolate	Cinnamon
English Toffee	Lemon Drop	Vanilla Creme
Berry	Hazelnut	Grape
Peppermint	Apricot	Orange
Chocolate Raspberry		

In the same way that powdered Stevia is far sweeter than other powdered sweeteners; liquid Stevia is sweeter than powdered Stevia. Begin with 1-2 drops, adding more for additional sweetness if desired.

Sweet n' Spicy Herbal Chai Tea
(makes 1 serving)

8-12 oz hot water
1 Spiced Chai tea bag
Stevia, to taste
1 tbsp fat-free milk (optional)

Place hot water and tea bag in cup, and steep tea for 3-5 minutes. Tea bag can be re-used for an additional cup later. Stir in Stevia and milk, if desired. Sip and savor. Additional suggestions: Pour over ice for a delicious iced chai tea. Keep a container of this tea in refrigerator to use for cooking or iced tea.

Crock-Pot Chai Tea
(makes 8 servings)

8 cups water
8 black tea bags
16 whole cloves
5 cinnamon sticks
8 slices fresh ginger
Stevia, to taste

Combine all ingredients in Crock Pot. Cover; cook on medium for 2 to 2-1/2 hours.

Strain mixture; discard solids. Serve warm or chilled. Add additional water to dilute before serving, if needed.

Flavored Coffee
(makes 1 serving)

8-12 oz hot water
1 flavored tea bag (mint, spice, raspberry, orange etc.)
1 heaping tsp instant coffee
Stevia, to taste
1 tbsp fat-free milk (optional)

Place hot water and tea bag in cup, and steep tea for 3 minutes (no longer). Tea bag can be re-used for an additional cup later. Stir in coffee, add Stevia and milk.

BLENDER BURSTS

Beth Golden, PhD, ND

BLENDER BURSTS

For each of the following, place all ingredients in blender and blend until smooth. Enjoy!

Strawberry Burst
(makes 1 serving: 1 fruit)

6 fresh strawberries
Stevia to taste
Fresh mint leaf (optional)
Ice cubes

Orange Burst
(makes 1 serving: 1 fruit)

1 orange, peeled and sectioned into pieces
1 tbsp fat-free milk
Stevia to taste
Pinch nutmeg (optional)
Ice cubes

Mojito Burst
(makes 1 serving)

6-8 oz soda, sparkling or mineral water
Juice of a lime (*see* Research, p. 185)
1-2 fresh mint leaves, crushed
Stevia, to taste
Ice cubes

Strawberry-Lemon Burst
(makes 1 serving: 1 fruit)

8 oz water
2 tbsp lemon juice
6 sliced strawberries*
Stevia to taste
Ice cubes

*If desired, reserve 1 slice or 1 whole strawberry for garnish.

DESSERTS

DESSERTS

Applesauce
(makes 4 servings: 1 fruit per serving)

4 large apples
2 tbsp apple cider vinegar
¾ cup water
¼ tsp cinnamon
Stevia to taste

Peel, core and dice apples. Place diced apples in mini-crock pot add water and cinnamon. Slow cook at 1 to 2 hours. (Or, place diced apples in sauce pan with water and cinnamon. Cook on LOW heat for 20 minutes.) When finished, mash with spoon or fork or place in blender on LOW to reach desired consistency. Serve warm or refrigerate and serve cold.

Baked Apple
(makes 1 serving: 1 fruit)

1 large apple
Stevia to taste
1 tbsp cinnamon
1 tbsp water
1 tsp cinnamon for garnish

With a sharp knife, scoop out center core of apple, leaving bottom in tact to form' cup'. Mix together Stevia and 1 tbsp cinnamon with water. Place apple on a sheet of foil. Pour mixture in center of apple and tighten foil securely up around apple. Bake at 350° for 30 to 45 minutes. Serve in a shallow dish and garnish with additional cinnamon.

Baked Apple Slices #1
(makes 1 serving: 1 fruit)

1 large Golden Delicious apple, sliced
⅛ tsp + 1 tsp cinnamon
Stevia to taste

Toss apple with ⅛ tsp cinnamon and Stevia; arrange in oven safe dish. Top with mixture of 1 tsp cinnamon and additional Stevia (optional). Bake at 350° until done.

Baked Apple Slices #2
(makes 4 servings: 1 fruit, 1 starch)

4 McIntosh apples
2 tbsp lemon juice
Stevia to taste
¼ tsp nutmeg
¼ tsp cinnamon
Pinch of cloves
Grissini bread sticks, crumbled (120 calories total)
1 tbsp water
Mint leaves, for garnish (optional)

Preheat oven to 350°. Peel and core apples, leaving whole. Slice apples horizontally into even ¼-inch-thick slices, brush with lemon juice. In separate bowl, mix Stevia, nutmeg, cinnamon, cloves and Grissini. Place ½ of apples in pie plate; sprinkle with ½ of spice mixture. Add remaining apples. Sprinkle with remaining spice mixture. Pour remaining lemon juice and water over apples. Cover and bake until tender and browned, and juices are thick (approx. 15 minutes). Remove cover during last 5 minutes of baking. Divide evenly onto 4 plates; garnish with mint leaves.

Strawberry Flower
(makes 1 serving: 1 fruit)

6 large strawberries, sliced
1 tsp cinnamon
Stevia, to taste (or 1-2 drops of chocolate
flavored Stevia)

Slice strawberries and place on a plate shaped like a flower. Mix cinnamon and Stevia and sprinkle over strawberries.

Chocolate Covered Strawberries
(Makes 1 serving: 1 fruit)

1 tbsp (heaping) pure cocoa powder
Stevia to taste
6 strawberries, rinsed and sliced

Mix cocoa and Stevia in small dish. Dip strawberries in mixture and enjoy!

Jamaican Grapefruit
(makes 1 serving: 1 fruit)

½ grapefruit pink or red
1 tsp cinnamon
Stevia to taste

Using a serrated knife, cut grapefruit in half. Place in an oven safe dish and bake for 2 minutes. Cut around center core & rind, and partition. Sprinkle with cinnamon and Stevia mixture.

Beth Golden, PhD, ND

FISH AND SEAFOOD ENTREES

FISH AND SEAFOOD ENTRIES *Acceptable White Fish in the recipes are*: Crab, Flounder, Halibut, Lobster, Haddock, Cod, Sole, Shrimp, Stone Crab, Tilapia, Swordfish, Bass, Pike, Brooke Trout, Jew Fish, John Dory or Snapper.

Zesty Garlic Shrimp
(makes 1 serving: 1 protein)

3 ½ oz shrimp, shelled and deveined
Pinch paprika
Pinch of sea salt
Pinch of ground pepper
2 tbsp chicken broth (*see* recipes, p. 161 & 162)
1 garlic clove, chopped
Pinch of crushed red pepper flakes (optional)
1 tbsp lemon juice
2 tsp parsley

Sprinkle shrimp with paprika, sea salt, pepper and set aside. Heat chicken broth, garlic and red pepper flakes in medium skillet. When garlic begins to brown, add shrimp, stirring until shrimp are firm to touch. Stir in lemon and parsley. Serve warm.

Florida Shrimp on the Grill
(makes 1 serving: 1 protein)

3 oz frozen, cooked shrimp
¼ tsp paprika
¼ tsp onion powder
¼ tsp garlic powder
Pinch of sea salt
Pinch of pepper
¼ fresh lemon
Skewer (previously soaked in water for 30 minutes)

Heat grill 5 minutes on high. Place frozen shrimp in water for 3 - 5 minutes to partially thaw. Remove and spear with a skewer. Sprinkle generous amounts of seasonings on both sides and grill over hot flame on each side just long enough to sear outside edges. Squeeze lemon over the top and serve.

Do not overcook! Serve with salad or vegetable, if desired.

Shrimp Stuffed Tomato
(makes 1 serving: 1 protein, 1 vegetable)

3 oz cooked shrimp, chopped
1 oz red onion, finely chopped
1 tbsp parsley
Pinch of Old Bay Seasoning
2 tbsp lemon juice
Sea salt, to taste
Pepper, to taste
1 small tomato

In small bowl, combine shrimp, onion, parsley, Old Bay, lemon juice, and sea salt and pepper. Cover and refrigerate 30-60 min. When ready to serve, cut off top of tomato. Scoop out and chop inside of tomato; discard seeds. Combine with shrimp mix, fill tomato and serve.

Portobello Mushrooms and Shrimp
(makes 2 servings: 1 protein, 1 vegetable, 1 fruit (wine)

6 oz large, cooked shrimp, shelled and deveined
2 large Portobello mushrooms, cleaned and sliced
¾ cup White Zinfandel, Champaign or Riesling wine
2 tbsp Bragg Liquid Aminos
1 medium onion, sliced and quartered
3 garlic cloves, peeled and sliced
1 tsp sea salt
¼ tsp dill weed
Pinch of poultry seasoning

Slice cleaned mushrooms into long thin slices and set aside. Heat wine on high in a medium sized non-stick skillet until comes to a boil, continue to cook another 2 -3 minutes to cook off alcohol.

Add Bragg's, onions, garlic and sea salt. Fast cook on medium high just until onions begin to get soft (don't overcook). Add sliced mushrooms, dill and poultry seasoning. Cover and reduce heat to MEDIUM/LOW. Cook an additional 6 – 10 minutes until mushrooms are done. Stir and check often. Add water if necessary near the end, but the mushrooms release water and you most likely will not need extra. Add cooked shrimp, stir well, cover and simmer until shrimp are warm. Remove from pan and serve. Enjoy!

ALTERNATIVE PROTEIN:
6 oz of ground, cooked white chicken or turkey breast

Shrimp with Broccoli and Onions
(makes 1 serving: 1 protein, 1 vegetable)

3 oz cooked shrimp, peeled and deveined
1 ½ oz onion, sliced
3 oz broccoli, cut into small pieces
2 tbsp lemon juice
2 tbsp water
Pinch of sea salt
Pinch of pepper (optional)

Place broccoli, onion, sea salt and water in medium sauté pan. Cook on MED/HI until just barely done. Add shrimp and season with sea salt and pepper.

Reduce heat to LOW and simmer 5 minutes.

Oriental Shrimp & Vegetables
(makes 4 servings: 1 protein, 1 vegetable per serving)

36 thawed jumbo shrimp, pre-cooked frozen (12 oz)
6 oz mushrooms, cleaned and sliced
5 oz broccoli pieces, frozen *or* fresh broccoli cut into 2" chunks
5 oz sweet yellow onion, cut into 2" chunks
4 medium garlic cloves, sliced
5 tbsp Bragg Liquid Aminos
5 tbsp water
¾ tsp sea salt
1 tbsp chopped ginger

Place frozen shrimp in cold water to partially thaw, quickly remove. Remove tails and set aside. Combine all remaining ingredients and cook covered on MED/HI for 6-8 minutes, stirring frequently and adding water if necessary.

Add shrimp, reduce heat to LOW and cook covered additional 3 minutes. Serve hot.

Zesty Crab Cakes
(makes 1 serving: 1 protein and 1 starch)

3 ½ oz crab (your preference)
Grissini or melba toast, finely ground (max 30 calories)
½ garlic clove, minced
¼ tsp onion powder
½ tbsp lemon juice
¼ tsp sea salt
¼ tsp ground pepper
¼ tsp dry mustard (⅛ tsp for milder flavor)
1 tsp parsley
1 tbsp skim milk
2 lemon wedges (for garnish)

Preheat oven to 350°. Mix all ingredients together and form patty. Refrigerate for 1 hour. Place in baking dish lined with parchment paper and bake for 10-15 minutes.

Southern Creole Catfish
(makes 1 serving: 1 protein, 1 vegetable)

3 ½ oz catfish or preferred fresh white fish
1 oz onion, minced
1-2 tsp Cajun seasoning (NO sugar)
½ cup water
Sea salt, to taste
Ground pepper, to taste (optional)
3 oz tomato, chopped

Preheat pan over MED-HI heat; add water. Cut fish into bite size pieces. Place fish in zip lock bag with minced onion and Cajun seasoning; shake fish to coat.

Cook for 3-4 minutes; add more water as needed. Add chopped tomato, reduce heat to MEDIUM and cook for additional 5 minutes or until tomatoes become tender and juices thicken.

Cod with Citrus Coleslaw
(makes 1 serving: 1 protein, 1 vegetable, 1 fruit)

3 ½ oz cod or preferred fresh white fish
1 cup water, divided
1 tbsp lemon juice
Pinch of sea salt
Pinch of pepper (optional)
3 sprigs chopped dill
4 oz shredded cabbage
1 tbsp Bragg Apple Cider Vinegar
¼ tsp celery seed
Stevia to taste
½ grapefruit, sliced in bite sized pieces

Place fish and ½ cup water in medium pan; drizzle with lemon juice. Season with sea salt, pepper and dill. Cook on medium heat until done.

In bowl, mix shredded cabbage, vinegar, celery seed, Stevia and grapefruit pieces. Serve with fish.

Spicy Cilantro Grouper
(makes 4 servings: 1 protein)

14 oz grouper or preferred fresh white fish
1 cup cilantro - pack cup with leaves
3 cloves minced garlic
2 tbsp lemon juice
1 tbsp crushed red pepper flakes
2 tbsp water (as needed)
Pinch of sea salt

Preheat oven to 400°. In food processor, combine cilantro, garlic, and red pepper flakes. Start to pulse and add water as necessary until reaches desired consistency. Place fish in baking dish or non-stick baking sheet. Drizzle lemon juice on fish, then top with cilantro mix.

Bake for 10-15 minutes depending on thickness, until fish flakes.

Tangy Cilantro Haddock
(makes 1 serving: 1 protein)

3 ½ oz haddock or preferred fresh white fish
¼ cup water
2 cloves garlic, minced
2 tbsp cilantro, finely chopped
½ of lemon
Pinch of sea salt
½ tsp lemon pepper
½ tsp paprika
Pinch of coriander
Pinch of cumin

Preheat oven to 450°. Rinse fish thoroughly then place on aluminum foil; place in baking pan. Crimp up edges of foil and add water. Spread garlic and cilantro on and around fish.

Squeeze lemon juice on fish, add sea salt and lemon pepper to taste; add paprika for color. Add additional spices.

Cover with foil and crimp edges to form a seal. Bake for 12-15 minutes. Fish will lose transparency and flake with fork when done.

Rosemary Halibut
(makes 1 serving: 1 protein)

3 ½ oz of halibut, or preferred fresh white fish
Pinch of rosemary, ground
Pinch of sea salt
Pinch of ground pepper (optional)
Pinch of garlic powder
¼-⅓ cup water
1 tbsp lemon juice

Sprinkle both sides of fish with spices. Place fish in nonstick sauté pan with water and lemon juice. Place lid on pan to steam fish.

Cook on MED/HI for 3-4 minutes per side. Fish is done when flakes easily with fork.

Citrus Mahi Mahi
(makes 1 serving: 1 protein)

3 ½ oz Mahi Mahi, or preferred fresh white fish
1 tbsp lemon juice
1 garlic clove, minced
¼ tsp dried thyme
¼ tsp dried dill
Pinch of pepper
Pinch of sea salt
1 tbsp Citrus Dressing (see recipe, p. 144)

Mix together lemon juice, garlic, thyme, dill, sea salt and pepper. Place fish in shallow dish, drizzle with citrus dressing mixture, turning to coat. Marinate at room temperature for 10 minutes.

Place in oven on center rack and broil approximately 6-8 minutes, depending on thickness. Fish will lose transparency and flake with fork when done.

Ginger Mahi Mahi
(makes 1 serving: 1 protein, 1 vegetable)

3 ½ oz Mahi Mahi or preferred fresh white fish
⅓ cup water
1 tsp garlic, minced
1 tsp ginger powder
Sea salt, to taste
Ground black pepper, to taste (optional)
4 oz sliced tomato
2 tbsp lemon juice

Preheat oven to 350°. Place fish on large sheet of aluminum foil, add water. Cover fish with garlic, ginger, sea salt and pepper. Place tomatoes on top of seasoned fish. Top with squeezed lemon juice. Close foil into a "pouch" so that top and ends are sealed. Bake for 10-12 minutes, depending on thickness, or until fish flakes.

Tantalizing Red Snapper
(makes 1 serving: 1 protein)

3 ½ oz red snapper
2 tbsp water
¼ tsp oregano
¼ tsp basil
Pinch of sea salt
1 tbsp lemon juice
Pinch of ground pepper,
1 garlic clove, crushed
¼ tsp paprika

Place fish on aluminum foil. In a bowl, mix all remaining ingredients. Baste fish with mixture and broil for 5 minutes, basting again after 2-3 minutes.

Turn fish over, baste again and cook for another 3 minutes, or until done.

Ginger Steamed Red Snapper
(makes 1 serving: 1 protein)

3 ½ oz red snapper, or preferred fresh white fish
1 tbsp fresh ginger, finely grated
¼ cup balsamic vinegar (*see* Research, p. 185)
Stevia to taste
Pinch of sea salt
Pinch of ground pepper
½ lemon, cut into wedges
Finish with a pinch of coriander

Add all seasonings to small skillet and cover with water to reach 2 inches; bring to a simmer. Add red snapper, cover and steam for about 10 minutes.

Mediterranean Red Snapper
(makes 1 serving: 1 protein, 1 vegetable)

3 ½ oz red snapper or preferred fresh white fish
2 tbsp lemon juice
1 tsp fresh ginger, finely minced
Pinch of sea salt
Pinch of pepper (optional)
4 oz fennel - cut into 1" pieces

Place fish in container with sealable lid; set aside. Place lemon juice in small bowl; stir in ginger, sea salt and pepper. Pour on fish, cover and marinate in refrigerator for 2 hours. Remove fish from marinade and place in glass baking dish lined with parchment paper. Place chopped fennel on top.

Cover dish with lid or aluminum foil and bake at 350° for 10-15 minutes or until fish flakes.

Tempting Tilapia
(makes 1 serving: 1 protein)

3 ½ oz tilapia or preferred fresh white fish
¼ tsp onion powder
¼ tsp garlic powder
Pinch of paprika
Pinch of sea salt
¼ tsp lemon juice

Generously sprinkle each seasoning on both sides of fish to coat well. Cover bottom of non-stick skillet with water and bring to boil. Add fish and cook on MED/HI for approximately 3-4 minutes, depending on thickness, turn and cook other side until fish flakes with fork and is no longer transparent. Add water as needed.

Remove fish, drizzle with juices from pan and serve.

Teriyaki Tilapia
(makes 1 serving: 1 protein)

3 ½ oz tilapia or preferred fresh white fish
1 tbsp Bragg Liquid Aminos
½ tsp Bragg Apple Cider Vinegar
2 cloves garlic, minced
⅛ tsp ginger powder

Mix all seasonings in zip lock bag or dish with lid. Add fish to coat. Seal and refrigerate for 30 minutes to 1 hour, turning once. Discard marinade and pat fish slightly dry. Place in aluminum and broil for 5-10 minutes, depending on thickness of fish.

TIP: If marinated in a zip lock bag you can simply flip the bag over in the refrigerator one or two times while marinating. When finished marinating, cut off one corner of bag and drain out marinade. Remove fish and pat slightly dry.

Lemon Tilapia
(makes 1 serving: 1 protein)

3 ½ oz tilapia or preferred fresh white fish
½ lemon, sliced
1 garlic clove, minced
Pinch of sea salt
¼ tsp ground pepper (optional)
½ tsp dry dill
½ cup water

Mix together lemon juice, garlic, sea salt, pepper and dill. Marinate fish in seasonings for 10 minutes and place in non-stick pan with water, cover and steam for 10 minutes.

Italian Herbed Rainbow Trout with Zucchini
(makes 1 serving: 1 protein, 1 vegetable)

3 ½ oz rainbow trout or preferred fresh white fish
1 cup water, divided
½ tsp sea salt
1 tsp Basil
½ tsp thyme
½ tsp oregano
Pinch of pepper (optional)
1 garlic clove chopped
2 tbsp lemon juice
1 lemon wedge
2 oz zucchini, chopped
2 oz tomato peeled and diced

Place ½ cup water and all seasonings in sauté pan on Medium heat. Add fish, drizzle with lemon juice. Add zucchini and tomato to pan; simmer until fish is thoroughly cooked, adding remaining water as needed. Pour juices over fish and garnish with lemon wedge.

Foil Baked White Fish
(makes 1 serving: 1 protein)

3 ½ oz preferred white fish
1 tbsp lemon juice
Pinch of garlic powder
Pinch of onion powder
Pinch of paprika
Pinch of sea salt
Pinch of pepper (optional)

Preheat oven to 350°. Place fish in aluminum foil, large enough to wrap around fish and seal. Drizzle with lemon juice. Season with garlic powder, onion powder, paprika, sea salt and pepper.

Bake until fish flakes with fork.

Wasabi Whitefish
(makes 1 serving: 1 protein)

3 ½ oz preferred white fish
¼ - ½ tsp wasabi powder
½ tsp ginger powder
Pinch of sea salt

In small dish, combine wasabi powder and ginger powder. Add fish and coat. Let stand for 15-30 minutes. Broil for 5-10 minutes, depending on thickness of fish. Splash with Bragg Liquid Aminos during the last minute of broiling.

Beth Golden, PhD, ND

MEAT AND POULTRY ENTREES

MEAT AND POULTRY ENTREES

Garlic Steak
(makes 1 serving: 1 protein)

3 ½ oz lean organic steak
(top sirloin or lean filet with all visual fat removed)
2 garlic cloves, cut into quarters
⅛ tsp garlic powder
⅛ tsp onion powder
¼ tsp thyme
Pinch of sea salt
Pinch of cracked pepper

Using something sharp, such as an ice pick or skewer, pierce holes in steak and insert garlic quarters directly into holes. Season steak with garlic powder, onion powder, sea salt and pepper. Broil in a preheated 450° oven (to sear in juices) with rack in the middle of the oven for approximately 6 to 8 minutes per side or until desired doneness. Can also be prepared on grill with LOW heat.

Balsamic Mustard Crusted Steak
(makes 1 serving: 1 protein)

3 ½ oz lean organic steak
 (top sirloin or lean filet with all visual fat removed)
1 tsp mustard powder
2 tsp balsamic vinegar (*see* Research, p. 185)
¼ tsp sea salt
½ tsp ground black pepper, optional
2 garlic cloves, minced
½ onion, minced

Line a broiler pan with foil and place steak on top. Mix all seasoning in a mixing bowl. Coat steak evenly with mustard mixture and let stand 10 minutes. Broil steak to desired temperature. (For medium-rare, 3 minutes per side if ½ inch thick or 4 minutes per side if ¾ inch thick.) Let stand 5 minutes before slicing and serving.

Rosemary Garlic Steak

(makes 1 serving: 1 protein)

3 ½ oz lean organic steak (top sirloin or lean filet-no fat)

1 tbsp Bragg Liquid Aminos

1 tbsp rosemary

1 tsp garlic paste (3-5 cloves minced)

½ tsp sea salt

½ tsp crushed red pepper

Place Bragg's in small dish, add steak and coat both sides well. In small bowl, combine rosemary, garlic, sea salt and red pepper. Rub on both sides of steak. Cover and refrigerate 4 hours to overnight. Spray grill lightly with Pam. Grill over medium flames to desired doneness.

Marinated Steak with Tomato and Onion
(makes 1 serving: 1 protein, 1 vegetable)

3 ½ oz lean organic steak (top sirloin or lean filet-no fat)
⅓ cup Bragg Apple Cider Vinegar
3 oz tomatoes, diced
1 oz onion, chopped
Stevia to taste

Seasonings:
2 tbsp dried oregano
3 tbsp garlic powder
¼ tsp sea salt
¼ tsp pepper
1 fresh thyme sprig, leaves only, chopped
Stevia to taste

Mix seasonings together and rub on steak. Marinate in refrigerator for 1 hour. In small bowl, mix together tomato and onion with vinegar and Stevia. Marinate for 1 hour. Broil or grill steak to desired doneness Place ½ of the tomato onion mixture onto a plate, top with cooked steak, then top with remaining tomato and onion mixture. Serve immediately.

Spicy Taco Salad
(makes 1 serving: 1 protein, 1 vegetable)

3 ½ oz ground lean organic steak (no hamburger)
¼ tsp sea salt
¼ cup + ⅓ cup water
¼ tsp Taco seasoning (*see* recipe, p. 169)
1 ½ oz diced tomato
½ oz onion, chopped
2 oz romaine lettuce

Combine ground steak with ¼ cup water and sea salt, and cook over MED/HI heat, stirring continually until beef is browned. Mix taco seasoning with ⅓ cup water and add to pan; simmer for 3-5 minutes. Top lettuce with beef, tomato and onion.

Mini Meat Loaf
(makes 1 serving: 1 protein, 1 starch, 1 vegetable)

3 ½ oz lean organic ground steak (no hamburger)
1 grissini OR Melba toast, ground into powder (total 30 calories)
1 garlic clove, minced
½ tsp dehydrated minced onion
¼ tsp allspice
⅛ tsp sage
Pinch of sea salt
Pinch of pepper
¼ cup sugar-free ketchup (*see* recipe, p. 145)
    (counts as 1 vegetable serving)
1 tsp skim milk

Preheat oven to 350°. In small bowl, combine all ingredients and form into small meat loaf. Place in glass dish lined with parchment paper, cover and bake approximately 20 minutes. Uncover dish, add ketchup to top and bake 5-10 additional minutes. Serve immediately.

Winter Chili
(makes 1 serving: 1 protein, 1 vegetable)

3 ½ oz ground lean organic steak or turkey (have steak selection ground by butcher)
1-2 garlic cloves, minced
1 oz onion chopped
½ cup water
2 oz tomatoes, diced
2 oz tomatoes, pureed
Seasonings:
½ tsp chili powder
½ tsp onion powder
¼ tsp oregano
¼ tsp sea salt
¼ tsp cumin
¼ tsp black pepper
Pinch cayenne (optional)
¼ tsp cilantro chopped
1 tsp Bragg Apple Cider Vinegar
Stevia to taste

Preheat pan over medium heat. Add minced garlic, onion and 1 tbsp of water to pan. Sauté for 2-3 minutes. Add more water as necessary. Increase heat to MED/HI. Add ground steak and sauté until brown - about 5 minutes.

Add all seasonings and cook an additional 3 minutes. Continue to add more water as necessary. Mix in tomatoes, puree and remaining water. Turn heat down to MED-LOW and simmer until it reaches desired consistency.

Can be frozen.

Half-Time Meatballs

(Makes 4 servings: One serving is 4 meatballs. 1 protein, 1 starch, 1 tbsp fat-free milk)

14 oz lean ground organic steak or ground turkey breast (no hamburger)
4 grissini bread sticks, ground into powder (120 calories total)
4 tbsp fat free milk
1 tbsp ground parsley
1 tsp onion powder
1 tsp basil
1 tsp oregano
½ tsp garlic, minced; 1 clove, finely chopped; or 1 tsp garlic powder
1 ½ tsp sea salt
Ground pepper, to taste

Preheat oven to 425°. In bowl, combine all ingredients. Form 16 meatballs. Place in glass baking dish lined with parchment paper or non-stick baking sheet and cook 10 minutes, turning halfway through cooking time. To brown more after cooking, broil for 1-2 minutes each side. Can be frozen.

Thai Cucumber Beef

(makes 1 serving: 1 protein, 1 vegetable)

3 ½ oz lean organic steak, thinly sliced

4 oz cucumber, peeled, seeded, sliced

½ tbsp lemon juice

¼ - ½ tbsp chopped cilantro

2 cloves minced garlic

1 tsp red pepper flakes

½ tsp ginger

½ tsp chopped lemon grass

¼ tsp ground pepper

2-3 tbsp water

¼ tsp sea salt

In small dish, combine cucumber, lemon juice and chopped cilantro. Toss, cover and place in refrigerator to marinate. Preheat pan over MED-HI heat. In small bowl, place steak, garlic, red pepper flakes, ginger, lemon grass and sea salt - coat steak well. Place steak in pan with water. Stir fry for 2-5 minutes. Serve immediately while hot over cold cucumbers.

Tangy Citrus Beef w/ Apples and Onions
(makes 1 serving: 1 protein, 1 vegetable, 1 fruit)

3 ½ oz lean organic veal or beef
Sea salt, to taste
Pepper, to taste
Pinch of chopped ginger
Pinch of garlic
½ cup + 3 tbsp water
½ tbsp lemon juice
1 apple, finely chopped
2 oz onion, sliced
2 oz mushrooms, sliced

Season pan with sea salt, pepper, ginger and garlic; add ½ cup water. Add meat and drizzle with lemon juice. Simmer until meat is nearly done. Add apple, onion, mushrooms and remaining water; cover and simmer for 2-3 minutes. Serve with juice from pan poured over meat.

Zesty Steak (or Chicken) w/ Tomatoes
(makes 1 serving: 1 protein, 1 vegetable)

3 ½ oz lean organic steak filet (or chicken breast)
4 oz tomatoes, diced
2 cloves garlic, minced
¼ tsp oregano
¼ tsp basil
¼ tsp chili powder
Sea salt, to taste
Ground pepper, to taste (optional)

Preheat oven to 325°. Place ½ of diced tomato in casserole dish lined with parchment paper. Add meat on top of tomato and top with minced garlic. In small bowl, toss remaining tomato with oregano, basil, chili powder, sea salt and pepper. Spoon on top of steak or chicken. Cover tightly with aluminum foil or with lid. Bake 45-60 minutes.

TIP: If using chicken, sear each side for 1-2 minutes in a frying pan with a dash of sea salt & pepper, just until browned. Then follow with same steps as above.

Steak w/Au Jus

(makes 1 serving: 1 protein, 1 vegetable)

3 ½ oz lean organic steak, thinly sliced

1 cup beef broth (*see* recipes, p. 163)

2 oz onions, sliced into rings

2 oz mushrooms, sliced

1 large cloves garlic, finely chopped

½ tsp thyme

½ tsp pepper

1 tsp Bragg Liquid Aminos

Preheat pan over medium heat. Add beef and splash of broth. Brown beef on each side then remove from pan. Using same pan, add onions, mushrooms and garlic. Cover and cook 5-10 minutes until tender. Add broth, thyme, pepper, Bragg's and sea salt. Bring to boil. Reduce heat and simmer 5-10 minutes.

Add steak and return to boil. Reduce heat and simmer additional 5-10 minutes each side. Serve steak and onions with au jus from pan.

Spicy Italian Chicken (or Turkey) Casserole
(makes 1 serving: 1 protein)

4 oz *sugar-free* stewed tomatoes
3 oz cooked chicken breast, cubed
¼ to ½ cup water
¼ tsp basil
¼ tsp oregano
¼ tsp Bragg Apple Cider Vinegar
Sea salt, to taste
Ground pepper, to taste
Pinch of chili pepper for a little extra spice (optional)
Stevia to taste

Mix all ingredients in a medium-to-large saucepan and simmer on LOW for 20-30 minutes.

Chicken (or Turkey) Chili
(makes 1 serving: 1 protein, 1 vegetable)

3 oz cooked chicken or turkey breast, freshly ground
4 oz crushed tomatoes
½ tbsp garlic, minced
¼ tsp cumin
¼ tsp oregano
¼ tsp red pepper flakes
¼ tsp chili powder
¼ tsp onion powder
¼ tsp coriander
⅛ tsp ground cloves
Pinch of sea salt
¼ tsp chopped cilantro
Tabasco® or other sugar-free, alcohol-free hot sauce, to taste (optional)

Preheat pan over MED/HI heat. Add all ingredients except for Tabasco® or hot sauce. Bring to a boil then reduce heat to simmer, cover and cook 30 minutes. Add Tabasco® or hot sauce right before serving.

Chicken (or Turkey) on the Grill
(one serving equals 3 oz chicken and 4 oz vegetables: 1 protein, 1 vegetable)

2-4 skinless, boneless chicken or turkey breasts
Sea salt and pepper
2 fresh thyme and 1 rosemary, chopped fine
1 large tomato, chopped
1 sweet yellow onion, chopped
5-6 mushrooms, chopped
2 garlic cloves, chopped
2 tbsp Bragg Liquid Aminos
Sea salt, to taste
Pepper, to taste

Season chicken with sea salt, pepper, thyme and rosemary; grill until done. Cut into bite size pieces and set aside. Toss vegetables and garlic together with Bragg's. Add sea salt and pepper to taste. Place vegetables in foil and wrap to seal. Place on grill and cook until desired tenderness. Mix vegetables together with chicken and serve.

Ginger Chicken (or Turkey) Wraps
(makes 1 serving: 1 protein, 1 vegetable)

3 ½ oz chicken or turkey breast
1 garlic clove
1 tbsp Bragg Apple Cider Vinegar
¼ tsp onion powder
Pinch of sea salt
Pinch of pepper
1 tsp fresh ginger, finely grated
½ cup water
4 oz green cabbage leaves
Stevia to taste

Add chicken and all seasonings to pan; cook until juices of chicken run clear. Add cabbage plus Stevia and cook until cabbage is slightly cooked. Divide chicken mixture and place on cabbage leaves. Roll into a wrap.

Bun-less Chicken (or Turkey) Burger
(makes 1 serving: 1 protein)

3 ½ oz of ground chicken or turkey breast
Pinch of ground pepper
Pinch of sea salt
¼ tsp onion powder
¼ tsp garlic powder
¼ tsp dry mustard

Mix all ingredients into ground chicken or turkey breast and mold into a patty. Grill or broil and serve with a salad or vegetable.

Orange Spiced Chicken (or Turkey) with Broccoli
(makes 1 serving: 1 protein, 1 vegetable, 1 fruit)

3 ½ oz chicken or turkey breast, cubed
4 oz broccoli
½ cup water, divided
Pinch of sea salt
¼ cup spiced chai tea (*see* recipe, p. 75; or from brewed tea bags)
1 orange, peeled and cut into small pieces

Add ¼ cup water and sea salt to pan. Bring to boil, add broccoli, cover and steam until desired tenderness; add water as needed. Set aside. Pour spiced chai tea into pan, add chicken and simmer on medium heat until chicken is tender. Mix broccoli, oranges, chicken and juice from pan and serve.

TIP: Can use beef or fish, too.

Curry Chicken (or Turkey) and Spinach
(makes 1 serving: 1 protein, 1 vegetable)

3 ½ oz chicken or turkey breast
½ tsp onion powder
1 garlic clove (minced)
½ tsp curry powder
½ cup chicken broth (*see* recipes, p. 161 & 162)
Pinch of sea salt
¼ tsp ground pepper
½ lime, cut into 2 wedges (*see* Research, p. 185)
4 oz spinach

Mix chicken, all seasonings, broth and juice from 1 lime wedge in pan. Cook chicken on MED until juices run clear (approximately 6-8 minutes). Add spinach for 1 minute and pour all ingredients into a bowl. Squeeze other lime wedge over mixture.

Oriental Chicken (or Turkey; or Shrimp) Wrap
(makes 1 serving: 1 protein, 1 vegetable)

3 oz cooked chicken or turkey breast or shrimp, chopped
1 large cabbage leaf (1 oz)
3 oz shredded cabbage
⅛ tsp onion salt
⅛ tsp garlic powder
1 tsp ginger
⅛ tsp Bragg Liquid Aminos
Stevia, to taste

Steam large cabbage leaf for 5 minutes. Move leaf over to side of steamer to make room to add shredded cabbage: steam both for 5 minutes. Set aside leaf. Place shredded cabbage in mixing bowl. Add chopped chicken, turkey or shrimp and seasonings. Mix well and wrap in cabbage leaf.

Chicken (or Shrimp) Stir Fry
(makes 4 servings: 1 protein, 1 vegetable)

12 oz cooked chicken breast or shrimp, diced
1 cup water, divided
1 tbsp Bragg's Liquid Aminos
1 tsp garlic powder
½ tsp ginger
7 oz broccoli flowerets, sliced
4 oz purple cabbage, chopped
2 oz sweet yellow onions, chopped
2 oz white or portabella mushrooms, sliced

Place ½ cup water, Bragg's, garlic powder and ginger in wok or sauté pan. Bring to simmer. Add all remaining vegetables except for mushrooms and mix well. Continue to stir until onions begin to become transparent. Add additional water as needed. Add chicken (or shrimp) and mushrooms and stir. Cook for additional 2-3 minutes. Can be equally portioned into 4 servings and refrigerated.

Oven Chicken (or Turkey) Salad
(makes 1 serving: 1 protein, 1 vegetable, 1 starch)

3 ½ oz chicken or turkey breast
¼ tsp onion powder
Pinch of sea salt
¼ tsp garlic powder
¼ tsp cayenne pepper (optional)
½ tsp poultry season (sugar-free)
Grissini or melba toast, finely ground (max 30 calories)
4 oz spinach or lettuce
Vinaigrette Dressing (*see* recipe, p. 143)

Preheat oven to 375°. Mix all seasonings and grissini/melba toast together and roll chicken in mixture until coated on all sides. Place on foil sheet and wrap up nice and tight. Place on a baking sheet and bake for 20-30 minutes. Cut chicken into small pieces and place on spinach or lettuce. Drizzle with vinaigrette dressing.

Grilled Chicken (or Turkey), Onions and Grapefruit Stir Fry
(makes 1 serving: 1 protein, 1 vegetable, 1 fruit)

3 ½ oz chicken or turkey breast, diced
4 oz red, yellow or white onion, sliced
½ grapefruit, peeled and cut into small pieces
Pinch of sea salt
Pinch of pepper
Stevia, to taste
3 tbsp + ¼ cup water

Place onions, 3 tbsp water, sea salt and pepper in skillet. Stir fry over medium heat until onions are transparent. Remove from pan and set aside. Add chicken and additional sea salt and pepper to pan; add remaining water. Simmer on medium heat until chicken is cooked through.

Place chicken with juice from pan in a bowl; add onions and grapefruit and toss.

Citrus Basil Chicken (or Turkey)
(makes 1 serving: 1 protein, 1 vegetable, 1 fruit)

3 ½ oz chicken or turkey breast, diced
Pinch of sea salt
¼ tsp pepper (optional)
½ cup water, as needed
Juice of ½ lemon
4 oz tomatoes, chopped
1 orange, peeled and cut into small pieces
Basil fresh chopped or dried, as desired

Place sea salt, pepper and 3 tbsp water in skillet on MED/HI heat. Add chicken. Drizzle with lemon juice. Add water 2 tbsp at a time if more moisture is needed. Cook chicken 2-3 minutes on each side. Add chopped tomatoes, chopped orange and basil. Simmer on LOW, allowing juices to marinate chicken. Turn chicken again to cook both sides evenly. When chicken is fully cooked, serve and enjoy.

Southwestern Salsa Chicken (or Turkey)
(makes 1 serving: 1 protein, 1 vegetable)

3 ½ oz chicken (or turkey) breast
Pinch of sea salt
Pinch of pepper
Cayenne Pepper, to taste (optional)
Stevia, to taste (optional)
1 cup water, as needed
2 oz tomato, chopped
½ oz onion, chopped
Spices:
2 sprigs fresh cilantro
Pinch of chili powder, cumin and coriander
1 ½ oz spinach or lettuce, shredded or diced

Coat chicken with sea salt, pepper, cayenne and Stevia; sauté chicken with ½ cup water 2-3 minutes on each side. Add tomato, onion and spices. Simmer until chicken is fully cooked. Remove and serve over spinach or lettuce.

ALTERNATIVE: Stir in chopped orange just before serving for a great citrus twist. (1 fruit)

SALAD DRESSINGS

SALAD DRESSINGS: Mix all ingredients, per recipe, in blender. Serve on 4 - 6 oz salad mixture. Store in refrigerator.

Vinaigrette Dressing

¼ cup Bragg Apple Cider Vinegar
½ cup water
½ tsp celery seed or garlic powder
½ tsp onion powder
½ tsp sea salt
1 garlic clove
Ground pepper, to taste (optional)
Stevia, to taste

Lemon Zing Dressing

¼ cup Bragg Apple Cider Vinegar
½ cup water
1 tbsp lemon juice
Pinch of oregano
Crushed chili peppers (optional)
Sea salt, to taste
Stevia, to taste

Zesty Vinaigrette Dressing

⅓ cup balsamic, red wine or rice vinegar (*see* Research, p. 185)
4 tbsp water or mineral oil
1 tsp dried thyme
¼ tsp sea salt
¼ tsp pepper
1 tsp dried basil
¼ tsp garlic powder

Citrus Dressing

¼ cup Bragg Apple Cider Vinegar
1 cup water
1 tbsp lemon juice
¼ tsp garlic powder
Pinch of sea salt
Pinch of pepper
Stevia, to taste

Dill Dressing

⅓ cup Bragg Apple Cider Vinegar
2 tsp water
1 tsp dried basil
1 tbsp dried dill
1 tsp garlic powder
Pinch of dry mustard
1 tsp onion powder
Pinch of sea salt
Stevia, to taste

Sweet n' Sour Vinaigrette Salad Dressing

1 tbsp Bragg Aminos
3 tbsp Bragg Apple Cider Vinegar
1-2 tbsp water
Pinch of sea salt
Pinch of pepper (optional)
Stevia, to taste

Luscious Lemon Dressing

4 tbsp lemon juice
3 tbsp water
2 garlic cloves, minced
Pinch of sea salt
Stevia, to taste

Mash garlic to near paste; add in all other ingredients and mix well. Refrigerate overnight. Makes 3 to 4 servings.

Sugar-Free Ketchup
(makes 1 ½ cups. One serving is 1 oz: 1 vegetable)

6 ounces tomato paste
½ cup Bragg Apple Cider Vinegar
½ cup water
2 tbsp onion, very finely minced
1 clove of garlic, very finely minced
Pinch of sea salt
⅛ tsp ground allspice (optional)
⅛ tsp ground cloves
⅛ tsp pepper
Stevia, to taste

Blend ingredients in blender until smooth. Put on LOW heat and simmer for 10 minutes. Pour into container with tight lid and store in refrigerator.

NOTE: To convert to Cocktail Sauce, add to taste: 1 tbsp lemon juice, 1 tbsp horseradish root and ½ tsp Bragg Liquid Amino.

SALADS

SALADS

Fennel and Celery Slaw Salad
(One serving is 4 oz: 1 vegetable)

1 bulb fennel, trimmed (reserve handful of fronds)
8 oz cabbage, shredded
¼ to ½ med onion, sliced (optional)
3 tbsp Bragg Apple Cider Vinegar (no sugar)
½ cup water
Stevia, to taste
4 ribs celery heart, thinly sliced
¼ tbsp celery salt
10 fresh basil leaves, finely chopped
¼ tsp sea salt
Pinch of ground pepper (optional)

Quarter fennel bulb, cut away core and slice thinly. Chop fennel fronds. Combine fennel with cabbage and onion. In small bowl, mix vinegar, water and Stevia. Add to mixture; toss well. Add celery and basil, toss to combine. Season with sea salt and pepper to taste. Simmer on LOW for 2-3 minutes then serve, or refrigerate 30-45 minutes before serving if cold salad is preferred.

Soy Sprout Salad (Namul)

(One serving is 4 oz - factor lettuce, if used: 1 vegetable)

3 cup water
12 oz fresh soy sprouts, rinsed
3 large scallions, thinly sliced
4 radishes, trimmed and thinly sliced (optional)
2 tbsp Bragg Liquid Amino Acids
1 ½ tbsp white or apple cider vinegar
Pinch of Stevia
Pinch of sea salt
Pinch of black pepper
Pinch of red pepper flakes (optional)

Bring 3 cup of water to a boil. Add soy sprouts and boil for about 2 minutes. Drain and rinse in cold water to stop cooking process. Combine all remaining ingredients, stir in sprouts and mix well. Include red pepper flakes only if you like everything hot! Cover and refrigerate for at 1-2 hours for flavors to meld. Serve cold, as a side dish or atop lettuce leaves.

Sweet Chunky Chicken Salad
(makes 1 serving: 1 protein, 1 vegetable, 1 fruit)

3 oz cooked chicken breast, diced
2 oz celery, diced
1 apple, dice all but 2 slices
2 tbsp lemon juice or 1 tbsp Bragg Apple Cider Vinegar
Dash of nutmeg
Dash of sea salt
⅛ tsp cinnamon
Stevia, to taste
2 oz lettuce

Place chicken, celery and apple in bowl. Add lemon juice, nutmeg and sea salt. Mix well. Sprinkle with cinnamon and Stevia. Chill for 30 minutes. Serve on lettuce and garnish with 2 apple slices.

Basil Marinated Spinach Chicken (or Turkey) Salad
(makes 1 serving: 1 protein, 1 vegetable, 1 fruit)

4 oz spinach, rinsed and dried
3 oz cooked chicken, chopped
½ grapefruit diced into bite size pieces
1 tbsp chopped basil, fresh if available
Vinaigrette dressing (*see* recipe, p. 143)

Place desired amount of vinaigrette dressing in large bowl, add chopped basil and stir. To enhance flavors add vanilla or raspberry Stevia drops. Add chicken, grapefruit and spinach. Toss and serve.

Strawberry Chicken (or Turkey) Salad
(makes 1 serving: 1 protein, 1 vegetable, 1 fruit)

4 oz lettuce, shredded
3 oz cooked chicken or turkey breast, chopped
6 strawberries, sliced
Vinaigrette Dressing (*see* recipe, p. 143)

Place lettuce in bowl with sliced strawberries. Add chicken and toss. Drizzle with vinaigrette; toss until lettuce is coated.

Veal with Spinach and Crunchy Apple Salad
(makes 1 serving: 1 protein, 1 vegetable, 1 fruit)

3 ½ oz veal or lean organic steak
   (top sirloin or filet; visible fat removed)
¼ cup spiced chai tea (*see* recipe, p. 75)
4 oz spinach leaves
1 apple cut into small pieces
Pinch of sea salt
Pinch of pepper

Pour spiced chai tea into pan with sea salt and pepper. Add veal and apples to pan and simmer on medium heat until veal is well cooked and apples are tender. Cut veal into bite sized pieces. Place spinach in a deep bowl. Add veal and apple to spinach and mix with any juices from the pan. (Adding more tea makes more juice which can be used as salad dressing)

TIP: Can also be made with chicken, turkey or shrimp.

Spicy Crab Cucumber Salad
(makes 1 serving: 1 protein, 1 vegetable)

4 oz cucumber - peeled, seeded, chopped
1 tbsp Bragg Liquid Aminos
½ tbsp Bragg Apple Cider Vinegar
2 tbsp water
½ tsp spicy mustard
½ tsp wasabi powder
½ clove of garlic, finely chopped (optional)
3 oz cooked crab, shredded (blue crab king or snow)

Combine aminos, vinegar, water, spicy mustard, and wasabi powder; mix well. Add cucumber and garlic, toss and serve with crab.

Tomato-Cucumber Salad
(makes 1 serving: 1 vegetable)

2 oz cucumber, diced
2 oz tomato, diced
2 tbsp balsamic vinegar
Pinch of sea salt
Stevia, to taste

Place cucumber and tomato in bowl. Cover with balsamic vinegar; sprinkle with sea salt. Enjoy!

Dieter's Deluxe Salad
(makes 1 serving: 1 vegetable)

2 oz romaine lettuce, chopped
1 oz purple cabbage, finely chopped
¾ oz mushrooms, sliced
¼ oz red onion, diced

Combine all ingredients and top with your favorite dressing. (see Dressings, p. 141)

Light & Zesty Salad
(makes 1 serving: 1 vegetable)

2 oz romaine lettuce, chopped
2 oz cauliflower, finely chopped
1 ½ oz tomatoes, diced
½ oz red onion

Combine all ingredients and top with your favorite dressing. (see Dressings, p. 141)

ALTERNATIVE: substitute cauliflower or tomatoes with cucumber, celery, radishes or broccoli.

Delicious Baby Spinach Salad
(makes 1 serving: 1 vegetable and 1 protein)

2 oz baby spinach, washed and dried
1 oz mushrooms, sliced
½ tbsp red onion, diced
½ tomato, chopped
3 oz cooked chicken breast, cubed or 1 egg and 3 egg whites, hard boiled and chopped

Combine all ingredients and top with your favorite dressing. (see Dressings, p. 141)

Beth Golden, PhD, ND

SOUPS, BROTHS, MARINADES AND SAUCES

SOUPS, BROTHS, MARINADES AND SAUCES

Beef & Asparagus Soup
(makes 1 serving: 1 protein, 1 vegetable)

3 oz cooked lean beef or veal, chopped
4 oz asparagus, chopped in ¼" sections
1 cup beef broth (*see* recipe, p. 163)
Seasonings, to taste
1 cup water
1 bay leaf

TIP: Snap off lower part of asparagus stem. The inedible part will snap off. To cook with the sweetest part of asparagus, peel outside of asparagus stem with a vegetable peeler before chopping into pieces.

Place beef broth in pan on MED heat. Bring to boil. Add beef and asparagus. Season to taste. Add additional water 1 tbsp at a time as needed. Simmer until asparagus is tender.

Turkey Cabbage Soup
(makes 1 serving: 1 protein, 1 vegetable)

3 oz cooked turkey breast, chopped
3 ½ oz cabbage, chopped
1 cup chicken broth (*see* recipes, p. 161 & 162)
1 tbsp minced onion
1 tsp sea salt
½ tsp dill
¼ tsp poultry seasoning
2 bay leaves
1 garlic clove, quartered
1 cup water

Place chicken broth in pan on MED heat. Bring to boil. Add all ingredients and simmer on MED/LOW until cabbage is tender.

ALTERNATIVES: A) Substitute lean organic chicken or beef for turkey; B) Use 2 oz celery and 2 oz cabbage and omit onion; or C) Add 1 tsp of lemon juice or vinegar with a pinch of Stevia to make a delicious sweet and sour broth.

Warm and Tantalizing Chicken Soup
(makes 3 Servings: 1 protein, 1 vegetable)

5 cup chicken broth (*see* recipes, p. 161 & 162)

10 ½ oz chicken or turkey breast, cut into cubes

1 large onion, cut into 2" chunks

2 celery stalks, cut into 1" pieces

1 zucchini, cubed

4 asparagus spears cut into 1' pieces (remove woody part of stem)

1 ½ tsp sea salt

¼ tsp dill

⅛ tsp poultry seasoning (sugar-free)

1 tsp onion powder

1 tsp garlic powder

Combine all ingredients in medium to large cooker. Heat on high just to the boiling point, reduce heat to LOW, cover and simmer 1 hour. Uncover and let set for 20 minutes, serve hot.

Savory Chicken or Turkey Broth
(makes 3 servings)

3 – 3 oz chicken or turkey breasts
4 cups water
2 tbsp parsley
½ onion diced finely
2 stalks celery diced finely
1 tsp garlic powder
½ tsp thyme
¼ tsp rosemary
½ tsp oregano
½ tsp basil
1 bay leaf
1 tsp sea salt
Pinch of black pepper

Bring water to a boil; add chicken, vegetables and seasonings. Boil for 20 minutes. Remove boiled chicken and serve or refrigerate for later. Strain out bay leaf and seasonings. Let broth cool to room temperature. Skim fat off surface (if any). Refrigerate broth. Once cold, skim the rest of the fat from the top (if any). Store in the refrigerator, or freeze for later use.

Homemade Chicken or Turkey Broth

1 chicken or turkey breast
8 cups water
5 tsp poultry season (*sugar-free*)
1 onion
4 garlic cloves
4 tsp black pepper
3 tsp sea salt
2 stalks celery
2 bay leaves
1 cheese cloth
1 string
1 coffee filter

Mix all herbs and place in cheese cloth. Tie with string to secure herbs and place in stock pot with water and chicken breast. Reduce heat and cook on MED/LOW for 15 minutes then simmer for 30 more minutes. Remove chicken; serve or save for later. Place a strainer lined with a coffee filter on top of a bowl. Slowly pour broth through strainer to help extract any fat from broth. If broth needs extra flavor, add ½ of spice mixture to 4 cups of boiling water and simmer for 30 minutes.

TIP: Broth is great as a base to cook vegetables such as onions, asparagus, broccoli or celery; use in all chicken recipes; or enjoy a cup of broth between or with lunch or dinner.

Homemade Beef Broth

4 pounds meaty beef stock bones
2 ½ quarts water
1 ½ teaspoon sea salt
2 bay leaves
1 medium onion, peeled and quartered
1 whole clove
2 cloves garlic, peeled
2 stalks celery with leaves
2 sprigs parsley

Put bones, water and remaining ingredients into a large soup kettle. Do not cover. Simmer for 3 hours. Remove meat from bones. Strain broth through a cheese cloth-lined colander. Cool slightly, refrigerate and then remove hardened fat from top of broth. Can be stored in refrigerator in covered container for up to 1 week or can be frozen in measured portions for easy use for up 6 months.

Makes about 2 ¼ quarts broth.

Orange Spice Meat Marinade
(makes 1 serving: 1 fruit)

Juice of 1 orange
Pinch of sea salt
Pinch of pepper
1-2 tbsp Bragg Apple Cider Vinegar
½ tsp sweet basil
Stevia, to taste

Squeeze the juice of 1 orange into a bowl. Add all remaining ingredients. Pour over 3 ½ oz of raw fish, beef or chicken. Marinate for 30 minutes or more. Cook meat on a grill or sauté in pan.

TIP: Marinade is also a terrific base to cook vegetables in. Remember to then count it as 1 fruit and 1 vegetable.

Marinara Sauce
(one serving is 4 oz: 1 vegetable)

2 large tomatoes
3 cups water + bowl of ice water
3 cloves garlic, minced
2 oz onions diced
½ tsp sea salt
¼ tsp pepper (optional)
1 tbsp parsley
5-6 fresh basil sprigs chopped
4 tbsp water

Fill small saucepan with 3 cups of water; bring to boil. Score skin of tomatoes in a few places with serrated knife. Blanch tomatoes in the boiling water for 1-2 minutes. Immediately transfer tomato to ice water to cool.

Remove tomato skin and discard. Preheat small non-stick saucepan over MED-HI heat. If chunky sauce is desired, discard stem and hand-crush tomato in sauce pan. If smoother sauce is preferred, discard stem and puree tomato in blender or food processor then add to pan.

Add garlic, onions, sea salt and pepper. Bring to LOW boil, then immediately reduce heat to LOW, cover & simmer for 15 minutes, stirring often to keep tomato from sticking. Turn heat up to MED. Add parsley and basil.

Cook 5-10 more minutes, stirring constantly. While cooking, start adding water 1 tbsp at a time until it reaches desired consistency.

SEASONINGS

SEASONINGS

Each of the seasonings is prepared as follows:

Place all ingredients in food processor or coffee grinder, grind to a powder and store in an air-tight container.

These seasonings can be used as a rub on chicken, steak or fish; to add more flavor when cooking vegetables; or to season salads and raw vegetables.

Greek Seasoning

2 tsp oregano

1 ½ tsp onion powder

1 ½ tsp garlic powder

½ tsp sea salt

1 tsp black pepper

1 tsp parsley

1 tsp basil

½ tsp cinnamon

½ tsp nutmeg

½ tsp thyme

Onion Soup Mix

½ cup dehydrated minced onion

1 tbsp onion powder

½ tbsp garlic powder

½ tsp dehydrated parsley

½ tsp celery seed

⅛ tsp dill

½ tsp sea salt

Pinch poultry seasoning

Zesty Onion Seasoning

½ cup minced dehydrated onions

⅛ tsp coriander

¼ tsp thyme

⅛ tsp oregano

⅛ tsp paprika

⅛ tsp black pepper, optional

⅛ tsp sea salt

Taco Seasoning

1 tbsp cumin

1 tbsp chili powder

2 tsp onion powder

1 tsp garlic powder

1 tsp paprika

½ tsp ground oregano

1 tsp sea salt

1 tbsp coriander

Steak Rub

2 tbsp dried parsley

¼ tsp thyme

¼ tsp garlic powder

Course ground sea salt

Course ground pepper

Cajun Seasoning

1 tbsp chili powder
1 tbsp paprika
1 tsp garlic powder
1 tsp onion powder
½ tsp dried oregano
½ tsp dried thyme
¼ tsp cayenne pepper
½ tsp freshly ground
pepper, optional
½ tsp sea salt

Southwestern Seasoning

2 tbsp chili powder
1 tbsp dried oregano
2 tbsp paprika
1 tbsp ground coriander
1 tbsp garlic powder
1 tsp sea salt
½ tsp ground cumin
1 tsp black pepper
1 tsp cayenne pepper
1 tsp ground red pepper

Curry Seasoning

1 tbsp turmeric

1 tbsp coriander

2 tsp paprika

1 tsp pepper

1 tsp cumin

1 tsp ginger

½ tsp cloves

½ tsp celery seed

½ tsp cayenne

Seafood Seasoning

1 tbsp ground bay leaves

2½ tsp celery seed

1½ tsp dry mustard

½ tsp black pepper, optional

¼ tsp ground nutmeg

½ tsp ground cloves

½ tsp ground ginger

½ tsp paprika

½ tsp red pepper, optional

⅛ tsp ground cardamom

⅛ tsp ground mace

1 tsp sea salt

Steak or Chicken BBQ Rub

2 tbsp paprika
1 tbsp black pepper
1 tbsp chili powder
½ tsp sea salt
⅛ tbsp ground cumin
Stevia, to taste

Tropical Chicken Rub

1 tbsp parsley
1 tsp cumin
1 tsp chili powder
½ tsp black pepper
½ tsp allspice
¼ tsp cinnamon
Pinch of sea salt

Combine all ingredients in zip-lock bag. Moisten chicken and then shake until well coated. Marinate for 20 minutes in refrigerator before grilling, baking or broiling. Makes enough for 2-4 servings of protein.

VEGETABLES

VEGETABLES

Tomato & Zucchini Casserole
(one serving is 4 oz: 1 vegetable)

2-3 medium tomatoes, sliced
2 medium zucchini, sliced
6 basil leaves chopped
1 tsp garlic powder
Pinch of sea salt
Pinch of pepper
Pinch of oregano
2 tbsp lemon juice

Preheat oven to 350°. Line bottom of small casserole dish with ½ of the tomatoes. Season with basil, garlic powder, sea salt, pepper, oregano and lemon juice. Follow with layer of ½ of zucchini; repeat seasoning.

Repeat layering with remaining tomatoes with seasoning and remaining zucchini with seasoning. Bake 30-45 minutes or until zucchinis are soft.

Roasted Brussels sprouts
(one serving is 4 oz: 1 vegetable)

1 package fresh Brussels sprouts
1 tbsp chopped fresh thyme leaves or 1 tsp dried
1 tbsp chopped fresh oregano leaves or 1 tsp dried
1 tsp garlic powder
Pinch of sea salt
Pinch of freshly ground black pepper
½ cup balsamic vinegar
Stevia, to taste

Preheat oven to 425°. Cut bottoms off Brussels sprouts and trim off any damaged outer leaves. Soak in bowl of cold water for a few minutes and drain well. Cut sprouts in half and place in roasting pan. Add thyme, oregano, garlic powder, sea salt, pepper and vinegar. Toss well to coat. Bake for 20 minutes. Stir and cook for additional 15 minutes, or until the Brussels sprouts are nicely browned and caramelized.

Roasted Asparagus
(one serving is 4 oz: 1 vegetable)

1 bunch fresh asparagus
1-2 cloves minced garlic
Pinch of sea salt
½ tsp parsley
½ - 1 cup water
Black pepper, to taste (optional)
1 tsp lemon juice (optional)

Preheat oven to 400°. Rinse asparagus and snap off inedible ends of stems. Spread spears on sheet of aluminum foil. Add all seasonings and water. Wrap ends of foil tightly to make a sealed 'pocket'. Roast 12-15 minutes.

ALTERNATIVE: Cook on the grill. Roast as above until done.

Lemon Ginger Asparagus
(one serving is 4 oz: 1 vegetable)

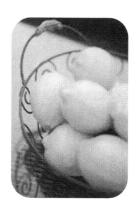

1 bunch of fresh asparagus
1 cup water, divided
½ tbsp fresh ginger root, minced
3 cloves minced garlic
1 tbsp lemon juice
1 tbsp Bragg Liquid Aminos
Pinch of black pepper (optional)

Snap off inedible ends of asparagus stems and discard. Snap spears into 2-3 pieces, set aside. Preheat pan over medium heat and add ½ cup water, garlic, Bragg Liquid Aminos and ginger. Cook for 2-3 minutes. Add asparagus and remaining water. Bring to boil for 5 minutes. Remove asparagus and top with pepper. Drizzle with lemon juice.

Savory Swiss Chard
(one serving is 4 oz: 1 vegetable)

1 large bunch Swiss chard, stemmed and coarsely chopped
¼ onion, diced
Freshly grated nutmeg, about ¼ tsp
½ tsp paprika or ground cumin
Sea salt and freshly ground black pepper, to taste
½ tsp Bragg Liquid Aminos
½ cup chicken broth (*see* recipes, p. 161 & 162)

Steam Swiss chard and onion until tender. Remove from steamer and transfer to sauté pan. Season with nutmeg and paprika or cumin, sea salt, pepper and Bragg's. Add chicken broth and simmer 5-10 minutes.

Lemon Garlic Chard
(one serving is 4 oz: 1 vegetable)

2 cups roughly chopped Swiss chard or spinach
2 garlic cloves, minced
4 tbsp water
1 tsp lemon juice
Pinch of sea salt
Pinch of pepper

Add garlic and 1 tbsp water to non-stick pan; sauté garlic until tender. Set garlic aside. Pour remaining water into pan and add chard. Cook over medium heat for about 5 minutes, tossing occasionally. Drain off excess juice and return to pan adding in sautéed garlic. Before serving, add lemon juice and a dash of sea salt and pepper.

Pickled Broccoli Stems
(one serving is 4 oz: 1 vegetable)

3 or 4 broccoli stems
2 tsp ground sea salt
1 or 2 garlic cloves, finely minced
½ cup water
2 tsp apple cider vinegar
Stevia, to taste

Peel skin from broccoli stems. Thinly slice stems diagonally, discarding tough end. Place broccoli and sea salt in glass jar with lid or covered plastic bowl. Leave in refrigerator overnight. Drain all salty water from sliced broccoli stems. Mix garlic, water and vinegar, add to broccoli and shake or stir well. Return to refrigerator for several hours or overnight before serving.

Roasted Cauliflower
(one serving is 4 oz: 1 vegetable)

1 head cauliflower (about 2 pounds), cut into bite-size flowerets (about 8 cups)
¼ cup Bragg Liquid Aminos
2 tbsp water
5 cloves garlic, roughly chopped
¼ tsp crushed red pepper
2 tsp sea salt
2 tsp roughly chopped fresh thyme leaves

Preheat oven to 450°. Toss cauliflower with Bragg's, garlic and red pepper on baking sheet; sprinkle with sea salt and thyme and toss again. Roast until golden and tender, about 20 minutes. Transfer to serving bowl and serve.

See additional tips and ideas for cauliflower on p. 17

Mushroom & Onion Sauté
(makes 1 serving: 1 vegetable)

½ cup water
1 tbsp Bragg Liquid Aminos
1 tbsp garlic powder
3 oz mushrooms, whole
1 oz red onion, sliced

On MED/HI heat, combine water, Bragg's and garlic powder in sauté pan.

Cover and bring to boil. Add mushrooms and red onion.

Toss mixture, cover and reduce heat to MED. Sauté for 3-4 minutes or until mushrooms begin to soften.

Remove from heat and slice mushrooms. Serve atop chicken, turkey or steak.

RESEARCH SECTION

RESEARCH SECTION

This section provides information about new foods and condiments that are being researched as alternatives and/or additions to the original Simeons' HCG Diet.

Since everyone is different, some HCG Dieters may find continued success with 1 or more of the changes, others may not. Success would be defined as when weight and inches continues to be lost at the rate expected; non-success would be defined as when weight or inches stop decreasing.

It is recommended that only one item be tried at a time so you are better able to monitor your results.

BALSAMIC & RED WINE VINEGAR: Since these vinegars are derived from grapes and are high in sugar, some people report adverse effects with weight loss with their use, others do not.

BRAGG LIQUID AMINOS: Bragg's can be purchased in a local health food store and is similar to soy sauce, however it contains no preservatives, no alcohol, is GMO and gluten free. This superior product is the preferred choice over soy sauce and many have used it successfully and experienced the same successful *weight and inch loss.*

GREEN BEANS: Most people continue to have great weight loss results including green beans as a vegetable choice, however occasionally, some have found their *weight and inch loss* stops or reduces.

KALE: Most people continue to have great weight loss results including kale as a vegetable choice, however occasionally, some have found their *weight and inch loss* stops or reduces.

LIMES: May be substituted for lemon juice in recipes or in water. Total daily combined juice of lemon and lime should not exceed the juice of 1 lemon *or* 1 lime.

RICE VINEGAR: Since rice vinegar is derived from rice (a starch), some people report adverse effects with weight loss with its use.

SOY SAUCE: Some people have found that the use of a *sugar-free* soy sauce does not affect their weight loss. Additional ingredients to watch for in soy sauce are wheat, gluten, molasses and MSG.

VEGETABLES: Dr. Simeon's original HCG Diet called for eating only one (1) vegetable at a time and he didn't state the serving amount. In our clinical tried, we witnesses no difference in loss if vegetable were or were not combined. Therefore, it is perfectly fine to combine vegetables as long as a serving equals approximately 4 – 6 ounces. ("water dense" vegetables weigh more)

WHITE WINE for cooking: As a base for specific dishes, ½ c of white zinfandel or the like is boiled on high briefly to remove the alcohol before adding additional ingredients in a recipe. *Counts as 1 fruit serving*.

VEGETARIAN PROTEIN SUBSTITUTES:

- 1 cup non-fat, sugar free, lecithin free Soy milk

- 1 cup non-fat, sugar free, lecithin free Almond milk (such as Pacific Brand)

- 1 cup non-fat cottage cheese

- 1 cup non-fat, sugar free plain goat or cow yogurt

**IMPORTANT: These items are much higher in carbohydrates and sugars than the original and revised Simeons HCG Diet calls for. Also, weight loss tends to be much slower due to the sugar and carb content of these protein substitutions.

Pounds & Inches

A NEW APPROACH TO OBESITY

BY: A.T.W. SIMEONS, M.D.
SALVATOR MUNDI INTERNATIONAL HOSPITAL
00152 - ROME
VIALE MURA GIANICOLENSI, 77

FOREWORD

This book discusses a new interpretation of the nature of obesity, and while it does not advocate yet another fancy slimming diet it does describe a method of treatment which has grown out of theoretical considerations based on clinical observation.

What I have to say is, in essence, the views distilled out of forty years of grappling with the fundamental problems of obesity, its causes, its symptoms, and its very nature. In these many years of specialized work, thousands of cases have passed through my hands and were carefully studied. Every new theory, every new method, every promising lead was considered, experimentally screened and critically evaluated as soon as it became known. But invariably the results were disappointing and lacking in uniformity.

I felt that we were merely nibbling at the fringe of a great problem, as, indeed, do most serious students of overweight. We have grown pretty sure that the tendency to accumulate abnormal fat is a very definite metabolic disorder, much as is, for instance, diabetes. Yet the localization and the nature of this disorder remained a mystery. Every new approach seemed to lead into a blind alley, and though patients were told that they are fat because they eat too much, we believed that this is neither the whole truth nor the last word in the matter.

Refusing to be side-tracked by an all too facile interpretation of obesity, I have always held that overeating is the result of the disorder, not its cause, and that we can make little headway until we can build for ourselves some sort of theoretical structure with which to explain the condition. Whether such a structure represents the truth is not important at this moment. What it must do is to give us an intellectually satisfying interpretation of what is happening in the obese body. It must also be able to withstand the onslaught of all hitherto known clinical facts and furnish a hard background against which the results of treatment can be accurately assessed.

To me this requirement seems basic, and it has always been the center of my interest. In dealing with obese patients it became a habit to register and order every clinical experience as if it were an odd looking piece of a jig-saw puzzle. And then, as in a jig saw puzzle, little clusters of fragments began to form, though they seemed to fit in nowhere. As the years passed these clusters grew bigger and started to amalgamate until, about sixteen years ago, a complete picture became dimly discernible. This picture was, and still is, dotted with gaps for which I cannot find the pieces, but I do now feel that a theoretical structure is visible as a whole.

With mounting experience, more and more facts seemed to fit snugly into the new framework, and then, when a treatment based on such speculations showed consistently satisfactory results, I was sure that some practical advance had been made, regardless of whether the theoretical interpretation of these results is correct or not.

The clinical results of the new treatment have been published in scientific journals and these reports have been generally well received by the profession, but the very nature of a scientific article does not permit the full presentation of new theoretical concepts nor is there room to discuss the finer points of technique and the reasons for observing them.

During the 16 years that have elapsed since I first published my findings, I have had many hundreds of inquiries from research institutes, doctors and patients. Hitherto I could only refer those interested to my scientific papers, though I realized that these did not contain sufficient information to enable doctors to conduct the new treatment satisfactorily. Those who tried were obliged to gain their own experience through the many trials and errors which I have long since overcome.

Doctors from all over the world have come to Italy to study the method, first hand in my clinic in the Salvator Mutidi International Hospital in Rome. For some of them the time they could spare has been too short to get a full grasp of the technique, and in any case the number of those whom I have been able to meet personally is small compared with the many requests for further detailed information which keep coming in. I have tried to keep up with these demands by correspondence, but the volume of this work has become unmanageable and that is one excuse for writing this book.

In dealing with a disorder in which the patient must take an active part in the treatment, it is, I believe, essential that he or she have an understanding of what is being done and why. Only then can there be intelligent cooperation between physician and patient. In order to avoid writing two books, one for the physician and another for the patient - a prospect which would probably have resulted in no book at all - I have tried to meet the requirements of both in a single book. This is a rather difficult enterprise in which I may not have succeeded. The expert will grumble about long-windedness while the lay-reader may occasionally have to look up an unfamiliar word in the glossary provided for him.

To make the text more readable I shall be unashamedly authoritative and avoid all the hedging and tentativeness with which it is customary to express new scientific concepts grown out of clinical experience and not as yet confirmed by clear-cut laboratory experiments. Thus, when I make what reads like a factual statement, the professional reader may have to translate into: clinical experience seems to suggest that such and such an observation might be tentatively explained by such and such a working hypothesis, requiring a vast amount of further research before the hypothesis can be considered a valid theory. If we can from the outset establish this as a mutually accepted convention, I hope to avoid being accused of speculative exuberance.

Obesity a Disorder

As a basis for our discussion we postulate that obesity in all its many forms is due to an abnormal functioning of some part of the body and that every ounce of abnormally accumulated fat is always the result of the same disorder of certain regulatory channels. Persons suffering from this particular disorder will get fat regardless of whether they eat excessively, normally or less than normal. A person who is free of the disorder will never get fat, even if he frequently overeats.

Those in whom the disorder is severe will accumulate fat very rapidly, those in whom it is moderate will gradually increase in weight and those in whom it is mild may be able to keep their excess weight stationary for long periods. In all these cases a loss of weight brought about by dieting, treatments with thyroid, appetite-reducing drugs, laxatives, violent exercise, massage, or baths is only temporary and will be rapidly regained as soon as the reducing regimen is relaxed. The reason is simply that none of these measures corrects the basic disorder.

While there are great variations in the severity of obesity, we shall consider all the different forms in both sexes and at all ages as always being due to the same disorder. Variations in form would then be partly a matter of degree, partly an inherited bodily constitution and partly the result of a secondary involvement of endocrine glands such as the pituitary, the thyroid, the adrenals or the sex glands. On the other hand, we postulate that no deficiency of any of these glands can ever directly produce the common disorder known as obesity.

If this reasoning is correct, it follows that a treatment aimed at curing the disorder must be equally effective in both sexes, at all ages and in all forms of obesity. Unless this is so, we are entitled to harbor grave doubts as to whether a given treatment corrects the underlying disorder. Moreover, any claim that the disorder has been corrected must be substantiated by the ability of the patient to eat normally of any food he pleases without regaining abnormal fat after treatment. Only if these conditions are fulfilled can we legitimately speak of curing obesity rather than of reducing weight.

Our problem thus presents itself as an enquiry into the localization and the nature of the disorder which leads to obesity. The history of this enquiry is a long series of high hopes and bitter disappointments.

The History of Obesity

There was a time, not so long ago, when obesity was considered a sign of health and prosperity in man and of beauty, amorousness and fecundity in women. This attitude probably dates back to Neolithic times, about 8000 years ago; when for the first time in the history of culture, man began to own property, domestic animals, arable land, houses, pottery and metal tools. Before that, with the possible exception of some races such as the Hottentots, obesity was almost non-existent, as it still is in all wild animals and most primitive races.

Today obesity is extremely common among all civilized races, because a disposition to the disorder can be inherited. Wherever abnormal fat was regarded as an asset, sexual selection tended to propagate the trait. It is only in very recent times that manifest obesity has lost some of its allure, though the cult of the outsize bust - always a sign of latent obesity - shows that the trend still lingers on.

The Significance of Regular Meals

In the early Neolithic times another change took place which may well account for the fact that today nearly all inherited dispositions sooner or later develop into manifest obesity. This change was the institution of regular meals. In pre-Neolithic times, man ate only when he was hungry and only as much as he required to still the pangs of hunger. Moreover, much of his food was raw and all of it was unrefined. He roasted his meat, but he did not boil it, as he had no pots, and what little he may have grubbed from the Earth and picked from the trees, he ate as he went along.

The whole structure of man's omnivorous digestive tract is, like that of an ape, rat or pig, adjusted to the continual nibbling of tidbits. It is not suited to occasional gorging as is, for instance, the intestine of the carnivorous cat family. Thus the institution of regular meals, particularly of food rendered rapidly, placed a great burden on modern man's ability to cope with large quantities of food suddenly pouring into his system from the intestinal tract.

The institution of regular meals meant that man had to eat more than his body required at the moment of eating so as to tide him over until the next meal. Food rendered easily digestible suddenly flooded his body with nourishment of which he was in no need at the moment. Somehow, somewhere this surplus had to be stored.

Three Kinds of Fat

In the human body we can distinguish three kinds of fat. The first is the structural fat which fills the gaps between various organs, a sort of packing material. Structural fat also performs such important functions as bedding the kidneys in soft elastic tissue, protecting the coronary arteries and keeping the skin smooth and taut. It also provides the springy cushion of hard fat under the bones of the feet, without which we would be unable to walk.

The second type of fat is a normal reserve of fuel upon which the body can freely draw when the nutritional income from the intestinal tract is insufficient to meet the demand. Such normal reserves are localized all over the body. Fat is a substance which packs the highest caloric value into the smallest space so that normal reserves of fuel for muscular activity and the maintenance of body temperature can be most economically stored in this form. Both these types of fat, structural and reserve, are normal, and even if the body stocks them to capacity this can never be called obesity.

But there is a third type of fat which is entirely abnormal. It is the accumulation of such fat, and of such fat only, from which the overweight patient suffers. This abnormal fat is also a potential reserve of fuel, but unlike the normal reserves it is not available to the body in a nutritional emergency. It is, so to speak, locked away in a fixed deposit and is not kept in a current account, as are the normal reserves.

When an obese patient tries to reduce by starving himself, he will first lose his normal fat reserves. When these are exhausted he begins to burn up structural fat, and only as a last resort will the body yield its abnormal reserves, though by that time the patient usually feels so weak and hungry that the diet is abandoned. It is just for this reason that obese patients complain that when they diet they lose the wrong fat. They feel famished and tired and their face becomes drawn and haggard, but their belly, hips, thighs and upper arms show little improvement. The fat they have come to detest stays on and the fat they need to cover their bones gets less and less. Their skin wrinkles and they look old and miserable. And that is one of the most frustrating and depressing experiences a human being can have.

Injustice to the Obese

When the obese patients are accused of cheating, gluttony, lack of will power, greed and sexual complexes, the strong become indignant and decide that modern medicine is a fraud and its represents fools, while the weak just give up the struggle in despair. In either case the result is the same: a further gain in weight, resignation to an abominable fate and the resolution at least to live tolerably the short span allotted to them - a fig for doctors and insurance companies.

Obese patients only feel physically well as long as they are stationary or gaining weight. They may feel guilty, owing to the lethargy and indolence always associated with obesity. They may feel ashamed of what they have been led to believe is a lack of control. They may feel horrified by the appearance of their nude body and the tightness of their clothes. But they have a primitive feeling of animal content which turns to misery and suffering as soon as they make a resolute attempt to reduce. For this there are sound reasons.

In the first place, more caloric energy is required to keep a large body at a certain temperature than to heat a small body. Secondly the muscular effort of moving a heavy body is greater than in the case of a light body. The muscular effort consumes calories which must be provided by food. Thus, all other factors being equal, a fat person requires more food than a lean one. One might therefore reason that if a fat person eats only the additional food his body requires he should be able to keep his weight stationary. Yet every physician who has studied obese patients under rigorously controlled conditions knows that this is not true. Many obese patients actually gain weight on a diet which is calorically deficient for their basic needs. There must thus be some other mechanism at work.

Glandular Theories

At one time it was thought that this mechanism might be concerned with the sex glands. Such a connection was suggested by the fact that many juvenile obese patients show an under-development of the sex organs. The middle-age spread in men and the tendency of many women to put on weight in the menopause seemed to indicate a causal connection between diminishing sex function and overweight. Yet, when highly active sex hormones became available, it was found that their administration had no effect whatsoever on obesity. The sex glands could therefore not be the seat of the disorder.

The Thyroid Gland

When it was discovered that the thyroid gland controls the rate at which body-fuel is consumed, it was thought that by administering thyroid gland to obese patients their abnormal fat deposits could be burned up more rapidly. This too proved to be entirely disappointing, because as we now know, these abnormal deposits take no part in the body's energy-turnover - they are inaccessibly locked away. Thyroid medication merely forces the body to consume its normal fat reserves, which are already depleted in obese patients, and then to break down structurally essential fat without touching the abnormal deposits. In this way a patient may be brought to the brink of starvation in spite of having a hundred pounds of fat to spare. **Thus any weight loss brought about by thyroid medication is always at the expense of fat of which the body is in dire need.**

While the majority of obese patients have a perfectly normal thyroid gland and some even have an overactive thyroid, one also occasionally sees a case with a real thyroid deficiency. In such cases, treatment with thyroid brings about a small loss of weight, but this is not due to the loss of any abnormal fat. It is entirely the result of the elimination of a mucoid substance, called myxedema, which the body accumulates when there is a marked primary thyroid deficiency. Moreover, patients suffering only from a severe lack of thyroid hormone never become obese in the true sense. Possibly also the observation that normal persons - though not the obese - lose weight rapidly when their thyroid becomes overactive may have contributed to the false notion that thyroid deficiency and obesity are connected. Much misunderstanding about the supposed role of the thyroid gland in obesity is still met with and it is now really high time that thyroid preparations be once and for all struck off the list of remedies for obesity. This is particularly so because giving thyroid gland to an obese patient whose thyroid is either normal or overactive, besides being useless, is decidedly dangerous.

The Pituitary Gland

The next gland to be falsely incriminated was the anterior lobe of the pituitary. This most important gland lies well protected in a bony capsule at the base of the skull. It has a vast number of functions in the body, among which is the regulation of all the other important endocrine glands. The fact that various signs of anterior pituitary deficiency are often associated with obesity raised the hope that the seat of the disorder might be in this gland. But although a large number of pituitary hormones have been isolated and many extracts of the gland prepared, not a single one or any combination of such factors proved to be of any value in the treatment of obesity. Quite recently, however, a fat-mobilizing factor has been found in pituitary glands, but it is still too early to say whether this factor is destined to play a role in the treatment of obesity.

The Adrenals

Recently, a Long series of brilliant discoveries concerning the working of the adrenal or suprarenal glands, small bodies which sit atop the kidneys, have created tremendous interest. This interest also turned to the problem of obesity when it was discovered that a condition which in some respects resembles a severe case of obesity - the so called Cushing's Syndrome - was caused by a glandular new-growth of the adrenals or by their excessive stimulation with ACTH, which is the pituitary hormone governing the activity of the outer rind or cortex of the adrenals.

When we learned that an abnormal stimulation of the adrenal cortex could produce signs that resemble true obesity, this knowledge furnished no practical means of treating obesity by decreasing the activity of the adrenal cortex. There is no evidence to suggest that in obesity there is any excess of adrenocortical activity; in fact, all the evidence points to the contrary. There seems to be rather a lack of adrenocortical function and a decrease in the secretion of ACTH from the anterior pituitary lobe.

So here again our search for the mechanism which produces obesity led us into a blind alley. Recently, many students of obesity have reverted to the nihilistic attitude that obesity is caused simply by overeating and that it can only be cured by under eating.

The Diencephalon or Hypothalamus

For those of us who refused to be discouraged there remained one slight hope. Buried deep down in the massive human brain there is a part which we have in common with all vertebrate animals the so-called diencephalon. It is a very primitive part of the brain and has in man been almost smothered by the huge masses of nervous tissue with which we think, reason and voluntarily move our body. The diencephalon is the part from which the central nervous system controls all the automatic animal functions of the body, such as breathing, the heartbeat, digestion, sleep, sex, the urinary system, the autonomous or vegetative nervous system and via the pituitary the whole interplay of the endocrine glands.

It was therefore not unreasonable to suppose that the complex operation of storing and issuing fuel to the body might also be controlled by the diencephalon. It has long been known that the content of sugar - another form of fuel - in the blood depends on a certain nervous center in the diencephalon. When this center is destroyed in laboratory animals, they develop a condition rather similar to human stable diabetes. It has also long been known that the destruction of another diencephalic center produces a voracious appetite and a rapid gain in weight in animals which never get fat spontaneously.

The Fat- bank

Assuming that in man such a center controlling the movement of fat does exist, its function would have to be much like that of a bank. When the body assimilates from the intestinal tract more fuel than it needs at the moment, this surplus is deposited in what may be compared with a current account. Out of this account it can always be withdrawn as required. All normal fat reserves are in such a current account, and it is probable that a diencephalic center manages the deposits and withdrawals.

When now, for reasons which will be discussed later, the deposits grow rapidly while small withdrawals become more frequent, a point may be reached which goes beyond the diencephalon's banking capacity. Just as a banker might suggest to a wealthy client that instead of accumulating a large and unmanageable current account he should invest his surplus capital, the body appears to establish a fixed deposit into which all surplus funds go but from which they can no longer be withdrawn by the procedure used in a current account. In this way the diencephalic "fat-bank" frees itself from all work which goes beyond its normal banking capacity. The onset of obesity dates from the moment the diencephalon adopts this labor-saving ruse. Once a fixed deposit has been established the normal fat reserves are held at a minimum, while every available surplus is locked away in the fixed deposit and is therefore taken out of normal circulation.

Three Basic Causes of Obesity

(1) The Inherited Factor

Assuming that there is a limit to the diencephalon's fat banking capacity, it follows that there are three basic ways in which obesity can become manifest. The first is that the fat-banking capacity is abnormally low from birth. Such a congenitally low diencephalic capacity would then represent the inherited factor in obesity. When this abnormal trait is markedly present, obesity will develop at an early age in spite of normal feeding; this could explain why among brothers and sisters eating the same food at the same table some become obese and others do not.

(2) Other Diencephalic Disorders

The second way in which obesity can become established is the lowering of a previously normal fat-banking capacity owing to some other diencephalic disorder. It seems to be a general rule that when one of the many diencephalic centers is particularly overtaxed; it tries to increase its capacity at the expense of other centers.

In the menopause and after castration the hormones previously produced in the sex-glands no longer circulate in the body. In the presence of normally functioning sex-glands their hormones act as a brake on the secretion of the sex-gland stimulating hormones of the anterior pituitary. When this brake is removed the anterior pituitary enormously increases its output of these sex-gland stimulating hormones, though they are now no longer effective. In the absence of any response from the non-functioning or missing sex glands, there is nothing to stop the anterior pituitary from producing more and more of these hormones. This situation causes an excessive strain on the diencephalic center which controls the function of the anterior pituitary. In order to cope with this additional burden the center appears to draw more and more energy away from other centers, such as those concerned with emotional stability, the blood circulation (hot flushes) and other autonomous nervous regulations, particularly also from the not so vitally important fat-bank.

The so called stable type of diabetes involves the diencephalic blood sugar regulating center. The diencephalon tries to meet this abnormal load by switching energy destined for the fat bank over to the sugar-regulating center, with the result that the fat-banking capacity is reduced to the point at which it is forced to establish a fixed deposit and thus initiate the disorder we call obesity. In this case one would have to consider the diabetes the primary cause of the obesity, but it is also possible that the process is reversed in the sense that a deficient or overworked fat-center draws energy from the sugar-center, in which case the obesity would be the cause of that type of diabetes in which the pancreas is not primarily involved. Finally, it is conceivable that in Cushing's syndrome those symptoms which resemble obesity are entirely due to the withdrawal of energy from the diencephalic fat-bank in order to make it available to the highly disturbed center which governs the anterior pituitary adrenocortical system.

Whether obesity is caused by a marked inherited deficiency of the fat-center or by some entirely different diencephalic regulatory disorder, its insurgence obviously has nothing to do with overeating and in either case obesity is certain to develop regardless of dietary restrictions. In these cases any enforced food deficit is made up from essential fat reserves and normal structural fat, much to the disadvantage of the patient's general health.

(3) The Exhaustion of the Fat-bank

But there is still a third way in which obesity can become established, and that is when a presumably normal fat-center is suddenly (with emphasis on suddenly) called upon to deal with an enormous influx of food far in excess of momentary requirements. At first glance it does seem that here we have a straight-forward case of overeating being responsible for obesity, but on further analysis it soon becomes clear that the relation of cause and effect is not so simple. In the first place we are merely assuming that the capacity of the fat center is normal while it is possible and even probable that the only persons who have some inherited trait in this direction can become obese merely by overeating.

Secondly, in many of these cases the amount of food eaten remains the same and it is only the consumption of fuel which is suddenly decreased, as when an athlete is confined to bed for many weeks with a broken bone or when a man leading a highly active life is suddenly tied to his desk in an office and to television at home. Similarly, when a person, grown up in a cold climate, is transferred to a tropical country and continues to eat as before, he may develop obesity because in the heat far less fuel is required to maintain the normal body temperature.

When a person suffers a long period of privation, be it due to chronic illness, poverty, famine or the exigencies of war, his diencephalic regulations adjust themselves to some extent to the low food intake. When then suddenly these conditions change and he is free to eat all the food he wants, this is liable to overwhelm his fat-regulating center. During the WWII about 6000 grossly underfed Polish refugees who had spent harrowing years in Russia were transferred to a camp in India where they were well housed, given normal British army rations and some cash to buy a few extras. Within about three months, 85% were suffering from obesity.

In a person eating coarse and unrefined food, the digestion is slow and only a little nourishment at a time is assimilated from the intestinal tract. When such a person is suddenly able to obtain highly refined foods such as sugar, white flour, butter and oil these are so rapidly digested and assimilated that the rush of incoming fuel which occurs at every meal may eventually overpower the diencephalic regulatory mechanisms and thus lead to obesity. This is commonly seen in the poor man who suddenly becomes rich enough to buy the more expensive refined foods, though his total caloric intake remains the same or is even less than before.

Psychological Aspects

Much has been written about the psychological aspects of obesity. Among its many functions the diencephalon is also the seat of our primitive animal instincts, and just as in an emergency it can switch energy from one center to another, so it seems to be able to transfer pressure from one instinct to another. Thus, a lonely and unhappy person deprived of all emotional comfort and of all instinct gratification except the stilling of hunger and thirst can use these as outlets for pent up instinct pressure and so develop obesity. Yet once that has happened, no amount of psychotherapy or analysis, happiness, company or the gratification of other instincts will correct the condition.

Compulsive Eating

No end of injustice is done to obese patients by accusing them of compulsive eating, which is a form of diverted sex gratification. Most obese patients do not suffer from compulsive eating; they suffer genuine hunger - real, gnawing, torturing hunger - which has nothing whatever to do with compulsive eating. Even their sudden desire for sweets is merely the result of the experience that sweets, pastries and alcohol will most rapidly of all foods allay the pangs of hunger. This has nothing to do with diverted instincts.

On the other hand, compulsive eating does occur in some obese patients, particularly in girls in their late teens or early twenties. Fortunately from the obese patients' greater need for food, it comes on in attacks and is never associated with real hunger, a fact which is readily admitted by the patients. They only feel a feral desire to stuff. Two pounds of chocolates may be devoured in a few minutes; cold, greasy food from the refrigerator, stale bread, leftovers on stacked plates, almost anything edible is crammed down with terrifying speed and ferocity.

I have occasionally been able to watch such an attack without the patient's knowledge, and it is a frightening, ugly spectacle to behold, even if one does realize that mechanisms entirely beyond the patient's control are at work. A careful enquiry into what may have brought on such an attack almost invariably reveals that it is preceded by a strong unresolved sex-stimulation, the higher centers of the brain having blocked primitive diencephalic instinct gratification. The pressure is then let off through another primitive channel, which is oral gratification. In my experience the only thing that will cure this condition is uninhibited sex, a therapeutic procedure which is hardly ever feasible, for if it were, the patient would have adopted it without professional prompting, nor would this in any way correct the associated obesity. It would only raise new and often greater problems if used as a therapeutic measure.

Patients suffering from real compulsive eating are comparatively rare. In my practice they constitute about 1-2%. Treating them for obesity is a heartrending job. They do perfectly well between attacks, but a single bout occurring while under treatment may annul several weeks of therapy. Little wonder that such patients become discouraged. In these cases I have found that psychotherapy may make the patient fully understand the mechanism, but it does nothing to stop it. Perhaps society's growing sexual permissiveness will make compulsive eating even rarer.

Whether a patient is really suffering from compulsive eating or not is hard to decide before treatment because many obese patients think that their desire for food (to them unmotivated) is due to compulsive eating, while all the time it is merely a greater need for food. The only way to find out is to treat such patients. Those that suffer from real compulsive eating continue to have such attacks, while those who are not compulsive eaters never get an attack during treatment.

Reluctance to Lose Weight

Some patients are deeply attached to their fat and cannot bear the thought of losing it. If they are intelligent, popular and successful in spite of their handicap, this is a source of pride. Some fat girls look upon their condition as a safeguard against erotic involvements, of which they are afraid. They work out a pattern of life in which their obesity plays a determining role and then become reluctant to upset this pattern and face a new kind of life which will be entirely different after their figure has become normal and often very attractive. They fear that people will like them - or be jealous - on account of their figure rather than be attracted by their intelligence or character only. Some have a feeling that reducing means giving up an almost cherished and intimate part of them. In many of these cases psychotherapy can be helpful, as it enables these patients to see the whole situation in the full light of consciousness. An affectionate attachment to abnormal fat is usually seen in patients who became obese in childhood, but this is not necessarily so.

In all other cases the best psychotherapy can do in the usual treatment of obesity is to render the burden of hunger and never-ending dietary restrictions slightly more tolerable. Patients who have successfully established an erotic transfer to their psychiatrist are often better able to bear their suffering as a secret labor of love.

There are thus a large number of ways in which obesity can be initiated, though the disorder itself is always due to the same mechanism, an inadequacy of the diencephalic fat-center and the laying down of abnormally fixed fat deposits in abnormal places. This means that once obesity has become established, it can no more be cured by eliminating those factors which brought it on than a fire can be extinguished by removing the cause of the conflagration. Thus a discussion of the various ways in which obesity can become established is useful from a preventative point of view, but it has no bearing on the treatment of the established condition. The elimination of factors which are clearly hastening the course of the disorder may slow down its progress or even halt it, but they can never correct it.

Not by Weight Alone

Weight alone is not a satisfactory criterion by which to judge whether a person is suffering from the disorder we call obesity or not. Every physician is familiar with the sylphlike lady who enters the consulting room and declares emphatically that she is getting horribly fat and wishes to reduce. Many an honest and sympathetic physician at once concludes that he is dealing with a "nut." If he is busy he will give her short shrift, but if he has time he will weigh her and show her tables to prove that she is actually underweight.

I have never yet seen or heard of such a lady being convinced by either procedure. The reason is that in my experience the lady is nearly always right and the doctor wrong. When such a patient is carefully examined one finds many signs of potential obesity, which is just about to become manifest as overweight. The patient distinctly feels that something is wrong with her, that a subtle change is taking place in her body, and this alarms her.

There are a number of signs and symptoms which are characteristic of obesity. In manifest obesity many and often all these signs and symptoms are present. In latent or just beginning cases some are always found, and it should be a rule that if two or more of the bodily signs are present, the case must be regarded as one that needs immediate help.

Signs and symptoms of obesity

The bodily signs may be divided into such as have developed before puberty, indicating a strong inherited factor, and those which develop at the onset of manifest disorder. Early signs are a disproportionately large size of the two upper front teeth, the first incisor, or a dimple on both sides of the sacral bone just above the buttocks. When the arms are outstretched with the palms upward, the forearms appear sharply angled outward from the upper arms. The same applies to the lower extremities. The patient cannot bring his feet together without the knees overlapping; he is, in fact, knock-kneed.

The beginning accumulation of abnormal fat shows as a little pad just below the nape of the neck, colloquially known as the Duchess' Hump. There is a triangular fatty bulge in front of the armpit when the arm is held against the body. When the skin is stretched by fat rapidly accumulating under it, it may split in the lower layers. When large and fresh such tears are purple, but later they are transformed into white scar-tissue. Such striation, as it is called, commonly occurs on the abdomen of women during pregnancy, but in obesity it is frequently found on the breasts, the hips and occasionally on the shoulders. In many cases striation is so fine that the small white lines are only just visible. They are always a sure sign of obesity, and though this may be slight at the time of examination such patients can usually remember a period in their childhood when they were excessively chubby.

Another typical sign is a pad of fat on the insides of the knees, a spot where normal fat reserves are never stored. There may be a fold of skin over the pubic area and another fold may stretch round both sides of the chest, where a loose roll of fat can be picked up between two fingers. In the male an excessive accumulation of fat in the breasts is always indicative, while in the female the breast is usually, but not necessarily, large. Obviously excessive fat on the abdomen, the hips, thighs, upper arms, chin and shoulders are characteristic, and it is important to remember that any number of these signs may be present in persons whose weight is statistically normal; particularly if they are dieting on their own with iron determination.

Common clinical symptoms which are indicative only in their association and in the frame of the whole clinical picture are: frequent headaches, rheumatic pains without detectable bony abnormality; a feeling of laziness and lethargy, often both physical and mental and frequently associated with insomnia, the patients saying that all they want is to rest; the frightening feeling of being famished and sometimes weak with hunger two to three hours after a hearty meal and an irresistible yearning for sweets and starchy food which often overcomes the patient quite suddenly and is sometimes substituted by a desire for alcohol; constipation and a spastic or irritable colon are unusually common among the obese, and so are menstrual disorders.

Returning once more to our sylphlike lady, we can say that a combination of some of these symptoms with a few of the typical bodily signs is sufficient evidence to take her case seriously. A human figure, male or female, can only be judged in the nude; any opinion based on the dressed appearance can be quite fantastically wide off the mark, and I feel myself driven to the conclusion that apart from frankly psychotic patients such as cases of anorexia nervosa; a morbid weight fixation does not exist. I have yet to see a patient who continues to complain after the figure has been rendered normal by adequate treatment.

The Emaciated Lady

I remember the case of a lady who was escorted into my consulting room while I was telephoning. She sat down in front of my desk, and when I looked up to greet her I saw the typical picture of advanced emaciation. Her dry skin hung loosely over the bones of her face, her neck was scrawny and collarbones and ribs stuck out from deep hollows. I immediately thought of cancer and decided to which of my colleagues at the hospital I would refer her. Indeed, I felt a little annoyed that my assistant had not explained to her that her case did not fall under my specialty. In answer to my query as to what I could do for her, she replied that she wanted to reduce. I tried to hide my surprise, but she must have noted a fleeting expression, for she smiled and said "I know that you think I'm mad, but just wait." With that she rose and came round to my side of the desk. Jutting out from a tiny waist she had enormous hips and thighs.

By using a technique which will presently be described, the abnormal fat on her hips was transferred to the rest of her body which had been emaciated by months of very severe dieting. At the end of a treatment lasting five weeks, she, a small woman, had lost 8 inches round her hips, while her face looked fresh and florid, the ribs were no longer visible and her weight was the same to the ounce as it had been at the first consultation.

Fat but not Obese

While a person who is statistically underweight may still be suffering from the disorder which causes obesity, it is also possible for a person to be statistically overweight without suffering from obesity. For such persons weight is no problem, as they can gain or lose at will and experience no difficulty in reducing their caloric intake. They are masters of their weight, which the obese are not. Moreover, their excess fat shows no preference for certain typical regions of the body, as does the fat in all cases of obesity. Thus, the decision whether a borderline case is really suffering from obesity or not cannot be made merely by consulting weight tables.

The Treatment of Obesity

If obesity is always due to one very specific diencephalic deficiency, it follows that the only way to cure it is to correct this deficiency. At first this seemed an utterly hopeless undertaking. The greatest obstacle was that one could hardly hope to correct an inherited trait localized deep inside the brain, and while we did possess a number of drugs whose point of action was believed to be in the diencephalons, none of them had the slightest effect on the fat-center. There was not even a pointer showing a direction in which pharmacological research could move to find a drug that had such a specific action. The closest approach were the appetite-reducing drugs - the amphetamines- ---- but these cured nothing.

A Curious Observation

Mulling over this depressing situation, I remembered a rather curious observation made many years ago in India. At that time we knew very little about the function of the diencephalon, and my interest centered round the pituitary gland. Proehlich had described cases of extreme obesity and sexual underdevelopment in youths suffering from a new growth of the anterior pituitary lobe, producing what then became known as Froehlich's disease. However, it was very soon discovered that the identical syndrome, though running a less fulminating course, was quite common in patients whose pituitary gland was perfectly normal. These are the so-called "fat boys" with long, slender hands, breasts any flat-chested maiden would be proud to possess, large hips, buttocks and thighs with striation, knock-knees and underdeveloped genitals, often with undescended testicles.

It also became known that in these cases the sex organs could be developed by giving the patients injections of a substance extracted from the urine of pregnant women, it having been shown that when this substance was injected into sexually immature rats it made them precociously mature. The amount of substance which produced this effect in one rat was called one International Unit, and the purified extract was accordingly called "Human Chorionic Gonadotrophin" whereby chorionic signifies that it is produced in the placenta and gonadotrophin that its action is sex gland directed.

The usual way of treating "fat boys" with underdeveloped genitals is to inject several hundred international Units twice a week. Human Chorionic Gonadotrophin which we shall henceforth simply call HCG is expensive and as "fat boys" are fairly common among Indians I tried to establish the smallest effective dose. In the course of this study three interesting things emerged. The first was that when fresh pregnancy-urine from the female ward was given in quantities of about 300 cc. by retention enema, as good results could be obtained as by injecting the pure substance. The second was that small daily doses appeared to be just as effective as much larger ones given twice a week. Thirdly, and that is the observation that concerns us here, when such patients were given small daily doses they seemed to lose their ravenous appetite though they neither gained nor lost weight. Strangely enough however, their shape did change. Though they were not restricted in diet, there was a distinct decrease in the circumference of their hips.

Fat on the Move

Remembering this, it occurred to me that the change in shape could only be explained by a movement of fat away from abnormal deposits on the hips, and if that were so there was just a chance that while such fat was in transition it might be available to the body as fuel. This was easy to find out, as in that case, fat on the move would be able to replace food. It should then be possible to keep a "fat boy" on a severely restricted diet without a feeling of hunger, in spite of a rapid loss of weight. When I tried this in typical cases of Froehlich's syndrome, I found that as long as such patients were given small daily doses of HCG they could comfortably go about their usual occupations on a diet of only 500 Calories daily and lose an average of about one pound per day. It was also perfectly evident that only abnormal fat was being consumed, as there were no signs of any depletion of normal fat. Their skin remained fresh and turgid, and gradually their figures became entirely normal. The daily administration of HCG appeared to have no side-effects other than beneficial ones.

From this point it was a small step to try the same method in all other forms of obesity. It took a few hundred cases to establish beyond reasonable doubt that the mechanism operates in exactly the same way and seemingly without exception in every case of obesity. I found that, though most patients were treated in the outpatients department, gross dietary errors rarely occurred. On the contrary, most patients complained that the two meals of 250 calories each were more than they could manage, as they continually had a feeling of just having had a large meal.

Pregnancy and Obesity

Once this trail was opened, further observations seemed to fall into line. It is well known that during pregnancy an obese woman can very easily lose weight. She can drastically reduce her diet without feeling hunger or discomfort and lose weight without in any way harming the child in her womb. It is also surprising to what extent a woman can suffer from pregnancy-vomiting without coming to any real harm.

Pregnancy is an obese woman's one great chance to reduce her excess weight. That she so rarely makes use of this opportunity is due to the erroneous notion, usually fostered by her elder relations, that she now has "two mouths to feed" and must "keep up her strength for the coming event". All modern obstetricians know that this is nonsense and the more superfluous fat that is lost the less difficult will be the confinement, though some still hesitate to prescribe a diet sufficiently low in calories to bring about a drastic reduction.

A woman may gain weight during pregnancy, but she never becomes obese in the strict sense of the word. Under the influence of the HCG which circulates in enormous quantities in her body during pregnancy, her diencephalic banking capacity seems to be unlimited, and abnormal fixed deposits are never formed. At confinement she is suddenly deprived of HCG, and her diencephalic fat-center reverts to its normal capacity. It is only then that the abnormally accumulated fat is locked away again in a fixed deposit. From that moment on she is again suffering from obesity and is subject to all its consequences.

Pregnancy seems to be the only normal human condition in which the diencephalic fat banking capacity is unlimited. It is only during pregnancy that fixed fat deposits can be transferred back into the normal current account and freely drawn upon to make up for any nutritional deficit. During pregnancy, every ounce of reserve fat is placed at the disposal of the growing fetus. Were this not so, an obese woman, whose normal reserves are already depleted, would have the greatest difficulties in bringing her pregnancy to full term. There is considerable evidence to suggest that it is the HCG produced in large quantities in the placenta which brings about this diencephalic change.

Though we may be able to increase the diencephalic fat banking capacity by injecting HCG, this does not in itself affect the weight, just as transferring monetary funds from a fixed deposit into a current account does not make a man any poorer; to become poorer it is also necessary that he freely spends the money which thus becomes available. In pregnancy the needs of the growing embryo take care of this to some extent, but in the treatment of obesity there is no embryo, and so a very severe dietary restriction must take its place for the duration of treatment.

Only when the fat which is in transit under the effect of HCG is actually consumed can more fat be withdrawn from the fixed deposits. In pregnancy it would be most undesirable if the fetus were offered ample food only when there is a high influx from the intestinal tract. Ideal nutritional conditions for the fetus can only be achieved when the mother's blood is continually saturated with food, regardless of whether she eats or not, as otherwise a period of starvation might hamper the steady growth of the embryo. It seems that HCG brings about this continual saturation of the blood, which is the reason why obese patients under treatment with HCG never feel hungry in spite of their drastically reduced food intake.

The Nature of Human Chorionic Gonadotrophin

HCG is never found in the human body except during pregnancy and in those rare cases in which a residue of placental tissue continues to grow in the womb in what is known as a chorionic epithelioma. It is never found in the male. The human type of chorionic gonadotrophin is found only during the pregnancy of women and the great apes. It is produced in enormous quantities, so that during certain phases of her pregnancy a woman may excrete as much as one million International Units per day in her urine - enough to render a million infantile rats precociously mature. Other mammals make use of a different hormone, which can be extracted from their blood serum but not from their urine. Their placenta differs in this and other respects from that of man and the great apes. This animal chorionic gonadotrophin is much less rapidly broken down in the human body than HCG, and it is also less suitable for the treatment of obesity.

As often happens in medicine, much confusion has been caused by giving HCG its name before its true mode of action was understood. It has been explained that gonadotrophin literally means a sex-gland directed substance or hormone, and this is quite misleading. It dates from the early days when it was first found that HCG is able to render infantile sex glands mature, whereby it was entirely overlooked that it has no stimulating effect whatsoever on normally developed and normally functioning sex-glands. No amount of HCG is ever able to increase a normal sex function. It can only improve an abnormal one and in the young hasten the onset of puberty. However, this has no direct effect. HCG acts exclusively at a diencephalic level and there brings about a considerable increase in the functional capacity of all those centers which are working at maximum capacity.

The Real Gonadotrophins

Two hormones known in the female as follicle stimulating hormone (FSH) and corpus luteum stimulating hormone (LSH) are secreted by the anterior lobe of the pituitary gland. These hormones are real gonadotrophins because they directly govern the function of the ovaries. The anterior pituitary is in turn governed by the diencephalon, and so when there is an ovarian deficiency the diencephalic center concerned is hard put to correct matters by increasing the secretion from the anterior pituitary of FSH or LSH, as the case may be. When sexual deficiency is clinically present, this is a sign that the diencephalic center concerned is unable, in spite of maximal exertion, to cope with the demand for anterior pituitary stimulation. When then the administration of HCG increases the functional capacity of the diencephalon, all demands can be fully satisfied and the sex deficiency is corrected.

That this is the true mechanism underlying the presumed gonadotrophic action of HCG is confirmed by the fact that when the pituitary gland of infantile rats is removed before they are given HCG, the latter has no effect on their sex-glands. HCG cannot therefore have a direct sex gland stimulating action like that of the anterior pituitary gonadotrophins, as FSH and LSH are justly called. The latter are entirely different substances from that which can be extracted from pregnancy urine and which, unfortunately, is called chorionic gonadotrophin. It would be no more clumsy, and certainly far more appropriate, if HCG were henceforth called chorionic diencephalotrophin.

HCG no Sex Hormone

It cannot be sufficiently emphasized that HCG is not a sex-hormone, that its action is identical in men, women, children and in those cases in which the sex-glands no longer function owing to old age or their surgical removal. The only sexual change it can bring about after puberty is an improvement of a pre-existing deficiency. But never stimulation beyond the normal. In an indirect way via the anterior pituitary, HCG regulates menstruation and facilitates conception, but it never virilizes a woman or feminizes a man. It neither makes men grow breasts nor does it interfere with their virility, though where this was deficient it may improve it. It never makes women grow a beard or developed a gruff voice. I have stressed this point only for the sake of my lay readers, because, it is our daily experience that when patients hear the word hormone they immediately jump to the conclusion that this must have something to do with the sex- sphere. They are not accustomed as we are, to think thyroid, insulin, cortisone, adrenalin etc, as hormones.

Importance and Potency of HCG

Owing to the fact that HCG has no direct action on any endocrine gland, its enormous importance in pregnancy has been overlooked and its potency underestimated. Though a pregnant woman can produce as much as one million units per day, we find that the injection of only 125 units per day is ample to reduce weight at the rate of roughly one pound per day, even in a colossus weighing 400 pounds, when associated with a 500-calorie diet. It is no exaggeration to say that the flooding of the female body with HCG is by far the most spectacular hormonal event in pregnancy. It has an enormous protective importance for mother and child, and I even go so far as to say that no woman, and certainly not an obese one, could carry her pregnancy to term without it.

If I can be forgiven for comparing my fellow-endocrinologists with wicked Godmothers, HCG has certainly been their Cinderella, and I can only romantically hope that its extraordinary effect on abnormal fat will prove to be its Fairy Godmother.

HCG has been known for over half a century. It is the substance which Aschheim and Zondek so brilliantly used to diagnose early pregnancy out of the urine. Apart from that, the only thing it did in the experimental laboratory was to produce precocious rats, and that was not particularly stimulating to further research at a time when much more thrilling endocrinological discoveries were pouring in from all sides, sweeping, HCG into the stiller back waters.

Complicating Disorders

Some complicating disorders are often associated with obesity, and these we must briefly discuss. The most important associated disorders and the ones in which obesity seems to play a precipitating or at least an aggravating role are the following: the stable type of diabetes, gout, rheumatism and arthritis, high blood pressure and hardening of the arteries, coronary disease and cerebral hemorrhage.

Apart from the fact that they are often - though not necessarily - associated with obesity, these disorders have two things in common. In all of them, modern research is becoming more and more inclined to believe that diencephalic regulations play a dominant role in their causation. The other common factor is that they either improve or do not occur during pregnancy. In the latter respect they are joined by many other disorders not necessarily associated with obesity. Such disorders are, for instance, colitis, duodenal or gastric ulcers, certain allergies, psoriasis, loss of hair, brittle fingernails, migraine, etc.

If HCG + diet do in the obese bring about those diencephalic changes which are characteristic of pregnancy, one would expect to see an improvement in all these conditions comparable to that seen in real pregnancy. The administration of HCG does in fact do this in a remarkable way.

Diabetes

In an obese patient suffering from a fairly advanced case of stable diabetes of many years duration in which the blood sugar may range from 300-400 mg, it is often possible to stop all anti-diabetes medication after the first few days of treatment. The blood sugar continues to drop from day to day and often reaches normal values in 2-3 weeks. As in pregnancy, this phenomenon is not observed in the brittle type of diabetes, and as some cases that are predominantly stable may have a small brittle factor in their clinical makeup, all obese diabetics have to be kept under a very careful and expert watch.

A brittle case of diabetes is primarily due to the inability of the pancreas to produce sufficient insulin, while in the stable type, diencephalic regulations seem to be of greater importance. That is possibly the reason why the stable form responds so well to the HCG method of treating obesity, whereas the brittle type does not. Obese patients are generally suffering from the stable type, but a stable type may gradually change into a brittle one, which is usually associated with a loss of weight. Thus, when an obese diabetic finds that he is losing weight without diet or treatment, he should at once have his diabetes expertly attended to. There is some evidence to suggest that the change from stable to brittle is more liable to occur in patients who are taking insulin for their stable diabetes.

Rheumatism

All rheumatic pains, even those associated with demonstrable bony lesions, improve subjectively within a few days of treatment, and often require neither cortisone nor salicylates. Again this is a well-known phenomenon in pregnancy, and while under treatment with HCG + diet the effect is no less dramatic. As it does not after pregnancy, the pain of deformed joints returns after treatment, but smaller doses of pain-relieving drugs seem able to control it satisfactorily after weight reduction. In any case, the HCG method makes it possible in obese arthritic patients to interrupt prolonged cortisone treatment without a recurrence of pain. This in itself is most welcome, but there is the added advantage that the treatment stimulates the secretion of ACTH in a physiological manner and that this regenerates the adrenal cortex, which is apt to suffer under prolonged cortisone treatment.

Cholesterol

The exact extent to which the blood cholesterol is involved in hardening of the arteries, high blood pressure and coronary disease is not as yet known, but it is now widely admitted that the blood cholesterol level is governed by diencephalic mechanisms. The behavior of circulating cholesterol is therefore of particular interest during the treatment of obesity with HCG. Cholesterol circulates in two forms, which we call free and esterified. Normally these fractions are present in a proportion of about 25% free to 75% esterified cholesterol, and it is the latter fraction which damages the walls of the arteries. In pregnancy this proportion is reversed and it may he taken for granted that arteriosclerosis never gets worse during pregnancy for this very reason.

To my knowledge, the only other condition in which the proportion of free to esterified cholesterol is reversed is during the treatment of obesity with HCG + diet, when exactly the same phenomenon takes place. This seems an important indication of how closely a patient under HCG treatment resembles a pregnant woman in diencephalic behavior.

When the total amount of circulating cholesterol is normal before treatment, this absolute amount is neither significantly increased nor decreased. But when an obese patient with abnormally high cholesterol and already showing signs of arteriosclerosis is treated with HCG, his blood pressure drops and his coronary circulation seems to improve, and yet his total blood cholesterol may soar to heights never before reached.

At first this greatly alarmed us. But when we saw that the patients came to no harm even if treatment was continued and we found the same in follow-up examinations undertaken some months after treatment was continued as we found in examinations undertaken some months before treatment. As the increase is mostly in the form of the not dangerous form of the free cholesterol, we gradually came to welcome the phenomenon. Today we believe that the rise is entirely due to the liberation of recent cholesterol deposits that have not yet undergone calcification in the arterial wall and is therefore highly beneficial.

Gout

An identical behavior is found in the blood uric acid level of patients suffering from gout. Predictably such patients get an acute and often severe attack after the first few days of HCG treatment but then remain entirely free of pain, in spite of the fact that their blood uric acid often shows a marked increase which may persist for several months after treatment. Those patients who have regained their normal weight remain free of symptoms regardless of what they eat, while those that require a second course of treatment get another attack of gout as soon as the second course is initiated. We do not yet know what diencephalic mechanisms are involved in gout; possibly emotional factors play a role, and it is worth remembering that the disease does not occur in women of childbearing age. We now give 2 tablets daily of ZYLOWRIC to all patients who give a history of gout and have a high blood uric acid level. In this way we can completely avoid attacks during treatment.

Blood Pressure

Patients, who have brought themselves to the brink of malnutrition by exaggerated dieting, laxatives etc, often have an abnormally low blood pressure. In these cases the blood pressure rises to normal values at the beginning of treatment and then very gradually drops, as it always does in patients with a normal blood pressure. Normal values are always regained a few days after the treatment is over. Of this lowering of the blood pressure during treatment the patients are not aware. When the blood pressure is abnormally high, and provided there are no detectable renal lesions, the pressure drops, as it usually does in pregnancy. The drop is often very rapid, so rapid in fact that it sometimes is advisable to slow down the process with pressure sustaining medication until the circulation has had a few days' time to adjust itself to the new situation. On the other hand, among the thousands of cases treated, we have never seen any incident which could be attributed to the rather sudden drop in high blood pressure.

When a woman suffering from high blood pressure becomes pregnant her blood pressure very soon drops, but after her confinement it may gradually rise back to its former level. Similarly, a high blood pressure present before HCG treatment tends to rise again after the treatment is over, though this is not always the case. But the former high levels are rarely reached, and we have gathered the impression that such relapses respond better to orthodox drugs such as Reserpine than before treatment.

Peptic Ulcers

In our cases of obesity with gastric or duodenal ulcers we have noticed a surprising subjective improvement in spite of a diet which would generally be considered most inappropriate for an ulcer patient. Here, too, there is a similarity with pregnancy, in which peptic ulcers hardly ever occur. However we have seen two cases with a previous history of several hemorrhages in which a bleeding occurred within 2 weeks of the end of treatment.

Psoriasis, Fingernails, Hair Varicose Ulcers

As in pregnancy, psoriasis greatly improves during treatment but may relapse when the treatment is over. Most patients spontaneously report a marked improvement in the condition of brittle fingernails. The Loss of hair not infrequently associated with obesity is temporarily arrested, though in very rare cases an increased Loss of hair has been reported. I remember a case in which a patient developed a patchy baldness - so called alopecia areata - after a severe emotional shock, just before she was about to start an HCG treatment. Our dermatologist diagnosed the case as a particularly severe one, predicting that all the hair would be lost. He counseled against the reducing treatment, but in view of my previous experience and as the patient was very anxious not to postpone reducing, I discussed the matter with the dermatologist and it was agreed that, having fully acquainted the patient with the situation, the treatment should be started. During the treatment, which lasted four weeks, the further development of the bald patches was almost, if not quite, arrested; however, within a week of having finished the course of HCG, all the remaining hair fell out as predicted by the dermatologist. The interesting point is that the treatment was able to postpone this result but not to prevent it. The patient has now grown a new shock of hair of which she is justly proud.

In obese patients with large varicose ulcers we were surprised to find that these ulcers heal rapidly under treatment with HCG. We have since treated non obese patients suffering from varicose ulcers with daily injections of HCG on a normal diet with equally good results.

The "Pregnant" Male

When a male patient hears that he is about to be put into a condition which in some respects resembles pregnancy, he is usually shocked and horrified. The physician must therefore carefully explain that this does not mean that he will be feminized and that HCG in no way interferes with his sex. He must be made to understand that in the interest of the propagation of the species nature provides for a perfect functioning of the regulatory headquarters in the diencephalon during pregnancy and that we are merely using this natural safeguard as a means of correcting the diencephalic disorder which is responsible for his being overweight.

Technique

Warnings

I must warn the lay reader that what follows is mainly for the treating physician and most certainly not a do-it-yourself primer. Many of the expressions used mean something entirely different to a qualified doctor than that which their common use implies, and only a physician can correctly interpret the symptoms which may arise during treatment. Any patient who thinks he can reduce by taking a few "shots" and eating less is not only sure to be disappointed but may be heading for serious trouble. The benefit the patient can derive from reading this part of the book is a fuller realization of how very important it is for him to follow to the letter his physician's instructions.

In treating obesity with the HCG + diet method we are handling what is perhaps the most complex organ in the human body. The diencephalon's functional equilibrium is delicately poised, so that whatever happens in one part has repercussions in others. In obesity this balance is out of kilter and can only be restored if the technique I am about to describe is followed implicitly. Even seemingly insignificant deviations, particularly those that at first sight seem to be an improvement, are very liable to produce most disappointing results and even annul the effect completely. For instance, if the diet is increased from 500 to 600 or 700 Calories, the Loss of weight is quite unsatisfactory. If the daily dose of HCG is raised to 200 or more units daily its action often appears to be reversed, possibly because larger doses evoke diencephalic counter-regulations. On the other hand, the diencephalon is an extremely robust organ in spite of its unbelievable intricacy. From an evolutionary point of view it is one of the oldest organs in our body and its evolutionary history dates back more than 500 million years. This has tendered it extraordinarily adaptable to all natural exigencies, and that is one of the main reasons why the human species was able to evolve. What its evolution did not prepare it for were the conditions to which human culture and civilization now expose it.

History taking

When a patient first presents himself for treatment, we take a general history and note the time when the first signs of overweight were observed. We try to establish the highest weight the patient has ever had in his life (obviously excluding pregnancy), when this was, and what measures have hitherto been taken in an effort to reduce.

It has been our experience that those patients who have been taking thyroid preparations for Long periods have a slightly Lower average Loss of weight under treatment with HCG than those who have never taken thyroid. This is even so in those patients who have been taking thyroid because they had an abnormally low basal metabolic rate. In many of these cases the low BMR is not due to any intrinsic deficiency of the thyroid gland, but rather to a lack of diencephalic stimulation of the thyroid gland via the anterior pituitary lobe. We never allow thyroid to be taken during treatment, and yet a BMR which was very low before treatment is usually found to be normal after a week or two of HCG + diet. Needless to say, this does not apply to those cases in which a thyroid deficiency has been produced by the surgical removal of a part of an overactive gland. It is also most important to ascertain whether the patient has taken diuretics (water eliminating pills) as this also decreases the weight Loss under the HCG regimen.

Returning to our procedure, we next ask the patient a few questions to which he is held to reply simply with "yes" or "no". These questions are: Do you suffer from headaches? rheumatic pains? menstrual disorders? constipation? breathlessness or exertion? swollen ankles? Do you consider yourself greedy? Do you feel the need to eat snacks between meals?

The patient then strips and is weighed and measured. The normal weight for his height, age, skeletal and muscular build is established from tables of statistical averages, whereby in women it is often necessary to make an allowance for particularly large and heavy breasts. The degree of overweight is then calculated, and from this the duration of treatment can be roughly assessed on the basis of an average Loss of weight of a little less than a pound, say 300-400 grams-per injection, per day. It is a particularly interesting feature of the HCG treatment that in reasonably cooperative patients this figure is remarkably constant, regardless of sex, age and degree of overweight.

The Duration of Treatment

Patients who need to lose 15 pounds (7 kg.) or less require 26 days treatment with 23 daily injections. The extra three days are needed because all patients must continue the 500-calorie diet for three days after the last injection. This is a very essential part of the treatment, because if they start eating normally as Long as there is even a trace of HCG in their body they put on weight alarmingly at the end of the treatment. After three days when all the HCG has been eliminated this does not happen, because the blood is then no Longer saturated with food and can thus accommodate an extra influx from the intestines without increasing its volume by retaining water.

We never give a treatment lasting less than 26 days, even in patients needing to lose only 5 pounds. It seems that even in the mildest cases of obesity the diencephalon requires about three weeks rest from the maximal exertion to which it has been previously subjected in order to regain fully its normal fat-banking capacity. Clinically this expresses itself, in the fact that, when in these mild cases, treatment is stopped as soon as the weight is normal, which may be achieved in a week, it is much more easily regained than after a full course of 23 injections.

As soon as such patients have lost all their abnormal superfluous fat, they at once begin to feel ravenously hungry with continued injections. This is because HCG only puts abnormal fat into circulation and cannot, in the doses used, liberate normal fat deposits; indeed, it seems to prevent their consumption. As soon as their statistically normal weight is reached, these patients are put on 800-1000 calories for the rest of the treatment. The diet is arranged in such a way that the weight remains perfectly stationary and is thus continued for three days after the 23rd injection. Only then are the patients free to eat anything they please except sugar and starches for the next three weeks.

Such early cases are common among actresses, models, and persons who are tired of obesity, having seen its ravages in other members of their family. Film actresses frequently explain that they must weigh less than normal. With this request we flatly refuse to comply, first, because we undertake to cure a disorder, not to create a new one, and second, because it is in the nature of the HCG method that it is self-limiting. It becomes completely ineffective as soon as all abnormal fat is consumed. Actresses with a slight tendency to obesity, having tried all manner of reducing methods, invariably come to the conclusion that their figure is satisfactory only when they are underweight, simply because none of these methods remove their superfluous fat deposits. When they see that under HCG their figure improves out of all proportion to the amount of weight lost, they are nearly always content to remain within their normal weight-range.

When a patient has more than 15 pounds to lose the treatment takes longer but the maximum we give in a single course is 40 injections, nor do we as a rule allow patients to lose more than 34 lbs. (15 Kg.) at a time. The treatment is stopped when either 34 lbs. have been lost or 40 injections have been given. **The only exception we make is in the case of grotesquely obese patients who may be allowed to lose an additional 5-6 lbs. if this occurs before the 40 injections are up.**

Immunity to HCG

The reason for limiting a course to 40 injections is that by then some patients may begin to show signs of HCG immunity. Though this phenomenon is well known, we cannot as yet define the underlying mechanism. Maybe after a certain length of time the body learns to break down and eliminate HCG very rapidly or possibly prolonged treatment leads to some sort of counter-regulation which annuls the diencephalic effect.

After 40 daily injections it takes about six weeks before this so called immunity is lost and HCG again becomes fully effective. Usually after about 40 injections patients may feel the onset of immunity as hunger which was previously absent. In those comparatively rare cases in which signs of immunity develops before the full course of 40 injections has been completed-say at the 35th injection- treatment must be stopped at once, because if it is continued the patients begin to look weary and drawn, feel weak and hungry and any further Loss of weight achieved is then always at the expense of normal fat. This is not only undesirable, but normal fat is also instantly regained as soon as the patient is returned to a free diet.

Patients who need only 23 injections may be injected daily, including Sundays, as they never develop immunity. In those that take 40 injections the onset of immunity can be delayed if they are given only six injections a week, leaving out Sundays or any other day they choose, provided that it is always the same day. On the days on which they do not receive the injections they usually feel a slight sensation of hunger. At first we thought that this might be purely psychological, but we found that when normal saline is injected without the patient's knowledge the same phenomenon occurs.

Menstruation

During menstruation no injections are given, but the diet is continued and causes no hardship; yet as soon as the menstruation is over, the patients become extremely hungry unless the injections are resumed at once. It is very impressive to see the suffering of a woman who has continued her diet for a day or two beyond the end of the period without coming for her injection and then to hear the next day that all hunger ceased within a few hours after the injection and to see her once again content, florid and cheerful. While on the question of menstruation it must be added that in teenaged girls the period may in some rare cases be delayed and essentially stop altogether. If then later this is artificially induced some weight may be regained.

Further Courses

Patients requiring the Loss of more than 34 lbs. must have a second or even more courses. *A second course can be started after an interval of not less than six weeks, though the pause can be more than six weeks.* When a third, fourth or even fifth course is necessary, the interval between courses should be made progressively longer. Between a second and third course eight weeks should elapse, between a third and fourth course twelve weeks, between a fourth and fifth course twenty weeks and between a fifth and sixth course six months. In this way it is possible to bring about a weight reduction of 100 lbs. and more if required without the least hardship to the patient.

In general, men do slightly better than women and often reach a somewhat higher average daily Loss. Very advanced cases do a little better than early ones, but it is a remarkable fact that this difference is only just statistically significant.

Conditions that must be accepted before treatment

On the basis of this data the probable duration of treatment can he calculated with considerable accuracy and this is explained to the patient. It is made clear to him that during the course of treatment he must attend the clinic daily to be weighed, injected and generally checked. All patients that live in Rome or have resident friends or relations with whom they can stay are treated as out-patients, but patients coming from abroad must stay in the hospital, as no hotel or restaurant can be relied upon to prepare the diet with sufficient accuracy. These patients have their meals, sleep, and attend the clinic in the hospital, but are otherwise free to spend their time as they please in the city and its surroundings sightseeing, sun-bathing or theater-going.

It is also made clear that between courses the patient gets no treatment and is free to eat anything he pleases except starches and sugar during the first 3 weeks. It is impressed upon him that he will have to follow the prescribed diet to the letter and that after the first three days this will cost him no effort, as he will feel no hunger and may indeed have difficulty in getting down the 500 Calories which he will be given. If these conditions are not acceptable the case is refused, as any compromise or half measure is bound to prove utterly disappointing to patient and physician alike and is a waste of time and energy.

Though a patient can only consider himself really cured when he has been reduced to his statically normal weight, we do not insist that he commit himself to that extent. Even a partial Loss of overweight is highly beneficial, and it is our experience that once a patient has completed a first course he is so enthusiastic about the ease with which the - to him surprising - results are achieved that he almost invariably comes back for more. There certainly can be no doubt that in my clinic more time is spent on damping over-enthusiasm than on insisting that the rules of the treatment be observed.

Examining the patient

Only when agreement is reached on the points so far discussed do we proceed with the examination of the patient. A note is made of the size of the first upper incisor, of a pad of fat on the nape of the neck, at the axilla and on the inside of the knees. The presence of striation, a suprapubic fold, a thoracic fold, angulation of elbow and knee joint, breast-development in men and women, edema of the ankles and the state of genital development in the male are noted.

Wherever this seems indicated we X-ray the sella turcica, as the bony capsule which contains the pituitary gland is called, measure the basal metabolic rate, X-ray the chest and take an electrocardiogram. We do a blood-count and a sedimentation rate and estimate uric acid, cholesterol, iodine and sugar in the fasting blood.

Gain before Loss

Patients whose general condition is low, owing to excessive previous dieting, must eat to capacity for about one week before starting treatment, regardless of how much weight they may gain in the process. One cannot keep a patient comfortably on 500 Calories unless his normal fat reserves are reasonably well stocked. **It is for this reason also that every case, even those that are actually gaining must eat to capacity of the most fattening food they can get down until they have had the third injection**. It is a fundamental mistake to put a patient on 500 Calories as soon as the injections are started, as it seems to take about three injections before abnormally deposited fat begins to circulate and thus become available.

We distinguish between the first three injections, which we call "non-effective" as far as the Loss of weight is concerned, and the subsequent injections given while the patient is dieting, which we call "effective". The average Loss of weight is calculated on the number of effective injections and from the weight reached on the day of the third injection which may be well above what it was two days earlier when the first injection was given.

Most patients who have been struggling with diets for years and know how rapidly they gain if they let themselves go are very hard to convince of the absolute necessity of gorging for at least two days, and yet this must be insisted upon categorically if the further course of treatment is to run smoothly. Those patients who have to be put on forced feeding for a week before starting the injections usually gain weight rapidly - four to six pounds in 24 hours is not unusual - but after a day or two this rapid gain generally levels off. In any case, the whole gain is usually lost in the first 48 hours of dieting. It is necessary to proceed in this manner because the gain re-stocks the depleted normal reserves, whereas the subsequent Loss is from the abnormal deposits only.

Patients in a satisfactory general condition and those who have not just previously restricted their diet start forced feeding on the day of the first injection. Some patents say that they can no Longer overeat because their stomach has shrunk after years of restrictions. While we know that no stomach ever shrinks, we compromise by insisting that they eat frequently of highly concentrated foods such as milk chocolate, pastries with whipped cream sugar, fried meats (particularly pork), eggs and bacon, mayonnaise, bread with thick butter and jam, etc. The time and trouble spent on pressing this point upon incredulous or reluctant patients is always amply rewarded afterwards by the complete absence of those difficulties which patients who have disregarded these instructions are liable to experience.

During the two days of forced feeding from the first to the third injection - many patients are surprised that contrary to their previous experience they do not gain weight and some even lose. The explanation is that in these cases there is a compensatory flow of urine, which drains excessive water from the body. To some extent this seems to be a direct action of HCG, but it may also be due to a higher protein intake, as we know that a **protein-deficient diet makes the body retain water**.

Starting treatment

In menstruating women, the best time to start treatment is immediately after a period. Treatment may also be started later, but it is advisable to have at least ten days in hand before the onset of the next period. Similarly, the end of a course should never be made to coincide with onset of menstruation. If things should happen to work out that way, it is better to give the last injection three days before the expected date of the menses so that a normal diet can he resumed at onset. Alternatively, at least three injections should be given after the period, followed by the usual three days of dieting. This rule need not be observed in such patients who have reached their normal weight before the end of treatment and are already on a higher caloric diet.

Patients who require more than the minimum of 23 injections and who therefore skip one day a week in order to postpone immunity to HCG cannot have their third injections on the day before the interval. Thus if it is decided to skip Sundays, the treatment can be started on any day of the week except Thursdays. Supposing they start on Thursday, they will have their third injection on Saturday, which is also the day on which they start their 500 calorie diet. They would then base no injection on the second day of dieting; this exposes them to an unnecessary hardship, as without the injection they will feel particularly hungry. Of course, the difficulty can be overcome by exceptionally injecting them on the first Sunday. If this day falls between the first and second or between the second and third injection, we usually prefer to give the patient the extra day of forced feeding, which the majority rapturously enjoy.

The Diet

The 500 calorie diet is explained on the day of the second injection to those patients who will be preparing their own food, and it is most important that the person who will actually cook is present - the wife, the mother or the cook, as the case may be. Here in Italy patients are given the following diet sheet.

Breakfast: Tea or coffee in any quantity without sugar. Only one tablespoonful of milk allowed in 24 hours. Saccharin or Stevia may be used.

Lunch: 1. 100 grams of veal, beef, chicken breast, fresh white fish, lobster, crab, or shrimp. All visible fat must be carefully removed before cooking, and the meat must be weighed raw. It must be boiled or grilled without additional fat.

Salmon, eel, tuna, herring, dried or pickled fish are not allowed. The chicken breast must be removed from the bird.

2. One type of vegetable only to be chosen from the following: spinach, chard, chicory, beet-greens, green salad, tomatoes, celery, fennel, onions, red radishes, cucumbers, asparagus, cabbage.

3. One breadstick (grissino) or one Melba toast.

4. An apple, orange, handful of strawberries or one-half grapefruit.

Dinner :   The same four choices as lunch.

The juice of one lemon daily is allowed for all purposes. Salt, pepper, vinegar, mustard powder, garlic, sweet basil, parsley, thyme, marjoram, etc., may be used for seasoning, but no oil, butter or dressing.

Tea, coffee, plain water, or mineral water are the only drinks allowed, but they may be taken in any quantity and at all times.

In fact, the patient should drink about 2 liters of these fluids per day. Many patients are afraid to drink so much because they fear that this may make them retain more water. This is a wrong notion as the body is more inclined to store water when the intake falls below its normal requirements.

The fruit or the breadstick may be eaten between meals instead of with lunch or dinner, but not more than four items listed for lunch and dinner may be eaten at one meal.

No medicines or cosmetics other than lipstick, eyebrow pencil and powder may he used without special permission

Every item in the list is gone over carefully, continually stressing the point that no variations other than those listed may be introduced. All things not listed are forbidden, and the patient is assured that nothing permissible has been left out. The 100 grams of meat must be scrupulously weighed raw after all visible fat has been removed. To do this accurately the patient must have a letter-scale, as kitchen scales are not sufficiently accurate and the butcher should certainly not be relied upon. Those not uncommon patients, who feel that even so little food is too much for them, can omit anything they wish.

There is no objection to breaking up the two meals. For instance having a breadstick and an apple for breakfast or before going to bed, provided they are deducted from the regular meals. The whole daily ration of two breadsticks or two fruits may not be eaten at the same time, nor can any item saved from the previous day be added on the following day. In the beginning patients are advised to check every meal against their diet sheet before starting to eat and not to rely on their memory. It is also worth pointing out that any attempt to observe this diet without HCG will lead to trouble in two to three days. We have had cases in which patients have proudly flaunted their dieting powers in front of their friends without mentioning the fact that they are also receiving treatment with HCG. They let their friends try the same diet, and when this proves to be a failure - as it necessarily must - the patient starts raking in unmerited kudos for superhuman willpower.

It should also be mentioned that two small apples weighing as much as one large one never the less have a higher caloric value and are therefore not allowed though there is no restriction on the size of one apple. Some people do not realize that chicken breast does not mean the breast of any other fowl, nor does it mean a wing or drumstick.

The most tiresome patients are those who start counting calories and then come up with all manner of ingenious variations which they compile from their little books. When one has spent years of weary research trying to make a diet as attractive as possible without jeopardizing the loss of weight, culinary geniuses who are out to improve their unhappy lot are hard to take.

Making up the Calories

The diet used in conjunction with HCG must not exceed 500 calories per day, and the way these calories are made up is of utmost importance. For instance, if a patient drops the apple and eats an extra breadstick instead, he will not be getting more calories but he will not lose weight. There are a number of foods, particularly fruits and vegetables, which have the same or even lower caloric values than those listed as permissible, and yet we find that they interfere with the regular Loss of weight under HCG, presumably owing to the nature of their composition. Pimiento peppers, okra, artichokes and pears are examples of this.

While this diet works satisfactorily in Italy, certain modifications have to be made in other countries. **For instance, American beef has almost double the caloric value of South Italian beef, which is not marbled with fat. This marbling is impossible to remove.** In America, therefore, low-grade veal should be used for one meal and fish (excluding all those species such as herring, mackerel, tuna, salmon, eel, etc., which have a high fat content, and all dried, smoked or pickled fish), chicken breast, lobster, crawfish, prawns or shrimp, crabmeat or kidneys for the other meal. Where the Italian breadsticks, the so-called grissini, are not available, one Melba toast may be used instead, though they are psychologically less satisfying. A Melba toast has about the same weight as the very porous grissini which is much more to look at and to chew.

When local conditions or the feeding habits of the population make changes necessary it must be borne in mind that the total daily intake must not exceed 500 calories if the best possible results are to be obtained, that the daily ration should contain 200 grams of fat-free protein and a very small amount of starch.

Just as the daily dose of HCG is the same in all cases, so the same diet proves to be satisfactory for a small elderly lady of leisure or a hard working muscular giant. Under the effect of HCG the obese body is always able to obtain all the calories it needs from the abnormal fat deposits, regardless of whether it uses up 1500 or 4000 per day. It must be made very clear to the patient that he is living to a far greater extent on the fat which he is losing than on what he eats.

Many patients ask why eggs are not allowed. The contents of two good sized eggs are roughly equivalent to 100 grams of meat, but unfortunately the yolk contains a large amount of fat, which is undesirable. Very occasionally we allow egg - boiled, poached or raw - to patients who develop an aversion to meat, but in this case they must add the white of three eggs to the one they eat whole. In countries where cottage cheese made from skimmed milk is available 100 grams may occasionally be used instead of the meat, but no other cheeses are allowed.

Vegetarians

Strict vegetarians such as orthodox Hindus present a special problem, because milk and curds are the only animal protein they will eat. To supply them with sufficient protein of animal origin they must drink 500 cc. of skimmed milk per day, though part of this ration can be taken as curds. As far as fruit, vegetables and starch are concerned, their diet is the same as that of non-vegetarians; they cannot be allowed their usual intake of vegetable proteins from leguminous plants such as beans or from wheat or nuts, nor can they have their customary rice. In spite of these severe restrictions, their average Loss is about half that of non-vegetarians, presumably owing to the sugar content of the milk.

Faulty Dieting

Few patients will take one's word for it that the slightest deviation from the diet has under HCG disastrous results as far as the weight is concerned. This extreme sensitivity has the advantage that the smallest error is immediately detectable at the daily weighing but most patients have to make the experience before they will believe it.

Persons in high official positions such as embassy personnel, politicians, senior executives, etc., who are obliged to attend social functions to which they cannot bring their meager meal must be told beforehand that an official dinner will cost them the Loss of about three days treatment, however careful they are and in spite of a friendly and would-be cooperative host. We generally advise them to avoid all around embarrassment, the almost inevitable turn of conversation to their weight problem and the outpouring of lay counsel from their table partners by not letting it be known that they are under treatment. They should take dainty servings of everything, bide what they can under the cutlery and book the gain which may take three days to get rid of as one of the sacrifices which their profession entails. Allowing three days for their correction, such incidents do not jeopardize the treatment, provided they do not occur all too frequently in which case treatment should be postponed to a socially more peaceful season.

Vitamins and anemia

Sooner or later most patients express a fear that they may be running out of vitamins or that the restricted diet may make them anemic. On this score the physician can confidently relieve their apprehension by explaining that every time they lose a pound of fatty tissue, which they do almost daily, only the actual fat is burned up; all the vitamins, the proteins, the blood, and the minerals which this tissue contains in abundance are fed back into the body. Actually, a low blood count not due to any serious disorder of the blood forming tissues improves during treatment, and we have never encountered a significant protein deficiency nor signs of a lack of vitamins in patients who are dieting regularly.

The First Days of Treatment

On the day of the third injection it is almost routine to hear two remarks. One is: "You know, Doctor, I'm sure it's only psychological, but I already feel quite different". So common is this remark, even from very skeptical patients that we hesitate to accept the psychological interpretation. The other typical remark is: "Now that I have been allowed to eat anything I want, I can't get it down. Since yesterday I feel like a stuffed pig. Food just doesn't seem to interest me anymore, and I am longing to get on with your diet". Many patients notice that they are passing more urine and that the swelling in their ankles is less even before they start dieting.

On the day of the fourth injection most patients declare that they are feeling fine. They have usually lost two pounds or more, some say they feel a bit empty but hasten to explain that this does not amount to hunger. Some complain of a mild headache of which they have been forewarned and for which they have been given permission to take aspirin.

During the second and third day of dieting - that is, the fifth and sixth injection-these minor complaints improve while the weight continues to drop at about double the usually overall average of almost one pound per day, so that a moderately severe case may by the fourth day of dieting have lost as much as 8- 10 lbs.

It is usually at this point that a difference appears between those patients who have literally eaten to capacity during the first two days of treatment and those who have not. The former feel remarkably well; they have no hunger, nor do they feel tempted when others eat normally at the same table. They feel lighter, more clear-headed and notice a desire to move quite contrary to their previous lethargy. Those who have disregarded the advice to eat to capacity continue to have minor discomforts and do not have the same euphoric sense of self-being until about a week later. It seems that their normal fat reserves require that much more time before they are fully stocked.

Fluctuations in weight Loss

After the fourth or fifth day of dieting the daily Loss of weight begins to decrease to one pound or somewhat less per day, and there is a smaller urinary output. Men often continue to lose regularly at that rate, but women are more irregular in spite of faultless dieting. There may be no drop at all for two or three days and then a sudden Loss which reestablishes the normal average. These fluctuations are entirely due to variations in the retention and elimination of water, which are more marked in women than in men.

The weight registered by the scale is determined by two processes not necessarily synchronized under the influence of HCG. Fat is being extracted from the cells, in which it is stored in the fatty tissue. When these cells are empty and therefore serve no purpose, the body breaks down the cellular structure and absorbs it, but breaking up of useless cells, connective tissue, blood vessels, etc., may lag behind the process of fat-extraction. When this happens the body appears to replace some of the extracted fat with water which is retained for this purpose. As water is heavier than fat the scales may show no Loss of weight, although sufficient fat has actually been consumed to make up for the deficit in the 500-Calorie diet. When such tissue is finally broken down, the water is liberated and there is a sudden flood of urine and a marked Loss of weight. This simple interpretation of what is really an extremely complex mechanism is the one we give those patients who want to know why it is that on certain days they do not lose, though they have committed no dietary error.

Patients who have previously regularly used diuretics as a method of reducing, lose fat during the first two or three weeks of treatment which shows in their measurements, but the scale may show little or no Loss because they are replacing the normal water content of their body which has been dehydrated. Diuretics should never be used for reducing.

Interruptions of Weight Loss

We distinguish four types of interruption in the regular daily Loss. The first is the one that has already been mentioned in which the weight stays stationary for a day or two, and this occurs, particularly towards the end of a course, in almost every case.

The Plateau

The second type of interruption we call a "plateau". A plateau lasts 4-6 days and frequently occurs during the second half of a full course, particularly in patients that have been doing well and who's overall average of nearly a pound per effective injection has been maintained. Those who are losing more than the average all have a plateau sooner or later. A plateau always corrects itself, but many patients who have become accustomed to a regular daily Loss get unnecessarily worried. No amount of explanation convinces them that a plateau does not mean that they are no Longer responding normally to treatment.

In such cases we consider it permissible, for purely psychological reasons, to break up the plateau. This can be done in two ways. One is a so-called "apple day". An apple-day begins at lunch and continues until just before lunch of the following day. The patients are given six large apples and are told to eat one whenever they feel the desire though six apples is the maximum allowed. During an apple-day no other food or liquids except plain water are allowed and of water they may only drink just enough to quench an uncomfortable thirst if eating an apple still leaves them thirsty. Most patients feel no need for water and are quite happy with their six apples. Needless to say, an apple-day may never be given on the day on which there is no injection. The apple-day produces a gratifying Loss of weight on the following day, chiefly due to the elimination of water. This water is not regained when the patients resume their normal 500-calorie diet at lunch, and on the following days they continue to lose weight satisfactorily.

The other way to break up a plateau is by giving a non-mercurial diuretic for one day. This is simpler for the patient but we prefer the apple-day as we sometimes find that though the diuretic is very effective on the following day it may take two to three days before the normal daily reduction is resumed, throwing the patient into a new fit of despair. It is useless to give either an apple-day or a diuretic unless the weight has been stationary for at least four days without any dietary error having been committed.

Reaching a Former Level

The third type of interruption in the regular Loss of weight may last much Longer - ten days to two weeks. Fortunately, it is rare and only occurs in very advanced cases, and then hardly ever during the first course of treatment. It is seen only in those patients who during some period of their lives have maintained a certain fixed degree of obesity for ten years or more and have then at some time rapidly increased beyond that weight. When then in the course of treatment the former level is reached, it may take two weeks of no Loss, in spite of HCG and diet, before further reduction is normally resumed.

Menstrual Interruption

The fourth type of interruption is the one which often occurs a few days before and during the menstrual period and in some women at the time of ovulation. It must also be mentioned that when a woman becomes pregnant during treatment - and this is by no means uncommon - she at once ceases to lose weight. An unexplained arrest of reduction has on several occasions raised our suspicion before the first period was missed. If in such cases, menstruation is delayed, we stop injecting and do a precipitation test five days later. No pregnancy test should be carried out earlier than five days after the last injection, as otherwise the HCG may give a false positive result.

Oral contraceptives may be used during treatment.

Dietary Errors

Any interruption of the normal Loss of weight which does not fit perfectly into one of those categories is always due to some possibly very minor dietary error. Similarly, any gain of more than 100 grams is invariably the result of some transgression or mistake, unless it happens on or about the day of ovulation or during the three days preceding the onset of menstruation, in which case it is ignored. In all other cases the reason for the gain must be established at once.

The patient who frankly admits that he has stepped out of his regimen when told that something has gone wrong is no problem. He is always surprised at being found out, because unless he has seen this himself he will not believe that a salted almond, a couple of potato chips, a glass of tomato juice or an extra orange will bring about a definite increase in his weight on the following day.

Very often he wants to know why extra food weighing one ounce should increase his weight by six ounces. We explain this in the following way: Under the influence of HCG the blood is saturated with food and the blood volume has adapted itself so that it can only just accommodate the 500 calories which come in from the intestinal tract in the course of the day. Any additional income, however little this may be, cannot be accommodated and the blood is therefore forced to increase its volume sufficiently to hold the extra food, which it can only do in a very diluted form. Thus it is not the weight of what is eaten that plays the determining role but rather the amount of water which the body must retain to accommodate this food.

This can be illustrated by mentioning the case of salt. In order to hold one teaspoonful of salt the body requires one liter of water, as it cannot accommodate salt in any higher concentration. Thus, if a person eats one teaspoonful of salt his weight will go up by more than two pounds as soon as this salt is absorbed from his intestine.

To this explanation many patients reply: Well, if I put on that much every time I eat a little extra, how can I hold my weight after the treatment? It must therefore be made clear that this only happens as Long as they are under HCG. When treatment is over, the blood is no Longer saturated and can easily accommodate extra food without having to increase its volume. Here again the professional reader will be aware that this interpretation is a simplification of an extremely intricate physiological process which actually accounts for the phenomenon.

Salt and Reducing

While we are on the subject of salt, I can take this opportunity to explain that we make no restriction in the use of salt and insist that the patients drink large quantities of water throughout the treatment. We are out to reduce abnormal fat and are not in the least interested in such illusory weight Losses as can be achieved by depriving the body of salt and by desiccating it. Though we allow the free use of salt, the daily amount taken should be roughly the same, as a sudden increase will of course be followed by a corresponding increase in weight as shown by the scale. An increase in the intake of salt is one of the most common causes for an increase in weight from one day to the next. Such an increase can be ignored, provided it is accounted for, it in no way influences the regular Loss of fat.

Water

Patients are usually hard to convince that the amount of water they retain has nothing to do with the amount of water they drink. When the body is forced to retain water, it will do this at all costs. If the fluid intake is insufficient to provide all the water required, the body withholds water from the kidneys and the urine becomes scanty and highly concentrated, imposing a certain strain on the kidneys. If that is insufficient, excessive water will be withdrawn from the intestinal tract, with the result that the feces become hard and dry. On the other hand if a patient drinks more than his body requires, the surplus is promptly and easily eliminated. Trying to prevent the body from retaining water by drinking less is therefore not only futile but even harmful.

Constipation

An excess of water keeps the feces soft, and that is very important in the obese, who commonly suffer from constipation and a spastic colon. While a patient is under treatment we never permit the use of any kind of laxative taken by mouth. We explain that owing to the restricted diet it is perfectly satisfactory and normal to have an evacuation of the bowel only once every three to four days and that, provided plenty of fluids are taken, this never leads to any disturbance. Only in those patients who begin to fret after four days do we allow the use of a suppository. Patients who observe this rule find that after treatment they have a perfectly normal bowel action and this delights many of them almost as much as their Loss of weight.

Investigating Dietary Errors

When the reason for a slight gain in weight is not immediately evident, it is necessary to investigate further. A patient who is unaware of having committed an error or is unwilling to admit a mistake protests indignantly when told he has done something he ought not to have done. In that atmosphere no fruitful investigation can be conducted; so we calmly explain that we are not accusing him of anything but that we know for certain from our not inconsiderable experience that something has gone wrong and that we must now sit down quietly together and try and find out what it was. Once the patient realizes that it is in his own interest that he play an active and not merely a passive role in this search, the reason for the setback is almost invariably discovered. Having been through hundreds of such sessions, we are nearly always able to distinguish the deliberate liar from the patient who is merely fooling himself or is really unaware of having erred.

Liars and Fools

When we see obese patients there are generally two of us present in order to speed up routine handling. Thus when we have to investigate a rise in weight, a glance is sufficient to make sure that we agree or disagree. If after a few questions we both feel reasonably sure that the patient is deliberately lying, we tell him that this is our opinion and warn him that unless he comes clean we may refuse further treatment. The way he reacts to this furnishes additional proof whether we are on the right track or not - we now very rarely make a mistake.

If the patient breaks down and confesses, we melt and are all forgiveness and treatment proceeds. Yet if such performances have to be repeated more than two or three times, we refuse further treatment. This happens in less than 1% of our cases. If the patient is stubborn and will not admit what he has been up to, we usually give him one more chance and continue even though we have been unable to find the reason for his gain. In many such cases there is no repetition, and frequently the patient does then confess a few days later after he has thought things over.

The patient who is fooling himself is the one who has committed some trifling, offense against the rules but who has been able to convince himself that this is of no importance and cannot possibly account for the gain in weight. Women seem particularly prone to getting themselves entangled in such delusions. On the other hand, it does frequently happen that a patient will in the midst of a conversation unthinkingly spear an olive or forget that he has already eaten his breadstick.

A mother preparing food for the family may out of sheer habit forget that she must not taste the sauce to see whether it needs more salt. Sometimes a rich maiden aunt cannot be offended by refusing a cup of tea into which she has put two teaspoons of sugar, thoughtfully remembering the patient's taste from previous occasions. Such incidents are legion and are usually confessed without hesitation, but some patients seem genuinely able to forget these lapses and remember them with a visible shock only after insistent questioning.

In these cases we go carefully over the day. Sometimes the patient has been invited to a meal or gone to a restaurant, naively believing that the food has actually been prepared exactly according to instructions. They will say: "Yes, now that I come to think of it the steak did seem a bit bigger than the one I have at home, and it did taste better; maybe there was a little fat on it, though I specially told them to cut it all away". Sometimes the breadsticks were broken and a few fragments eaten, and "Maybe they were a little more than one". It is not uncommon for patients to place too much reliance on their memory of the diet-sheet and start eating carrots, beans or peas and then to seem genuinely surprised when their attention is called to the fact that these are forbidden, as they have not been listed.

Cosmetics

When no dietary error is elicited we turn to cosmetics. Most women find it hard to believe that fats, oils, creams and ointments applied to the skin are absorbed and interfere with weight reduction by HCG just as if they had been eaten. This almost incredible sensitivity to even such very minor increases in nutritional intake is a peculiar feature of the HCG method. For instance, we find that persons who habitually handle organic fats, such as workers in beauty parlors, masseurs, butchers, etc. never show what we consider a satisfactory Loss of weight unless they can avoid fat coming into contact with their skin.

The point is so important that I will illustrate it with two cases. A lady who was cooperating perfectly suddenly increased half a pound. Careful questioning brought nothing to light. She had certainly made no dietary error nor had she used any kind of face cream, and she was already in the menopause. As we felt that we could trust her implicitly, we left the question suspended. Yet just as she was about to leave the consulting room she suddenly stopped, turned and snapped her fingers. "I've got it," she said. This is what had happened: She had bought herself a new set of make-up pots and bottles and, using her fingers, had transferred her large assortment of cosmetics to the new containers in anticipation of the day she would be able to use them again after her treatment.

The other case concerns a man who impressed us as being very conscientious. He was about 20 lbs. overweight but did not lose satisfactorily from the onset of treatment. Again and again we tried to find the reason but with no success, until one day he said: "I never told you this, but I have a glass eye. In fact, I have a whole set of them. I frequently change them, and every time I do that I put a special ointment in my eye socket. Do you think that could have anything to do with it?" As we thought just that, we asked him to stop using this ointment and from that day on his weight-loss was regular.

We are particularly averse to those modern cosmetics which contain hormones, as any interference with endocrine regulations during treatment must be absolutely avoided. Many women whose skin has in the course of years become adjusted to the use of fat containing cosmetics find that their skin gets dry as soon as they stop using them. In such cases we permit the use of plain mineral oil, which has no nutritional value. On the other hand, mineral oil should not be used in preparing the food, first because of its undesirable laxative quality, and second because it absorbs some fat-soluble vitamins, which are then lost in the stool. We do permit the use of lipstick, powder and such Lotions as are entirely free of fatty substances. We also allow brilliantine to be used on the hair but it must not be rubbed into the scalp. Obviously sun-tan oil is prohibited.

Many women are horrified when told that for the duration of treatment they cannot use face creams nor have facial massages. They fear that this and the Loss of weight will ruin their complexion. They can be fully reassured. Under treatment normal fat is restored to the skin, which rapidly becomes fresh and turgid, making the expression much more youthful. This is a characteristic of the HCG method which is a constant source of wonder to patients who have experienced or seen in others the facial ravages produced by the usual methods of reducing. An obese woman of 70 obviously cannot expect to have her pued face reduced to normal without a wrinkle, but it is remarkable how youthful her face remains in spite of her age.

The Voice

Incidentally, another interesting feature of the HCG method is that it does not ruin a singing voice. The typically obese prima donna usually finds that when she tries to reduce, the timbre of her voice is liable to change, and understandably this terrifies her. Under HCG this does not happen; indeed, in many cases the voice improves and the breathing invariably does. We have had many cases of professional singers very carefully controlled by expert voice teachers, and they have been so enthusiastic that they now frequently send us patients.

Other Reasons for a Gain

Apart from diet and cosmetics there can be a few other reasons for a small rise in weight. Some patients unwittingly take chewing gum, throat pastilles, vitamin pills, cough syrups etc., without realizing that the sugar or fats they contain may interfere with a regular Loss of weight. Sex hormones or cortisone in its various modern forms must be avoided, though oral contraceptives are permitted. In fact the only self-medication we allow aspirin for a headache, though headaches almost invariably disappear after a week of treatment, particularly if of the migraine type.

Occasionally we allow sleeping tablet or a tranquilizer, but patients should be told that while under treatment they need and may get less sleep. For instance, here in Italy where it is customary to sleep during the siesta which lasts from one to four in the afternoon most patients find that though they lie down they are unable to sleep.

We encourage swimming and sun bathing during treatment, but it should be remembered that a severe sunburn always produces a temporary rise in weight, evidently due to water retention. The same may be seen when a patient gets a common cold during treatment. Finally, the weight can temporarily increase - paradoxical though this may sound - after an exceptional physical exertion of Long duration leading to a feeling of exhaustion. A game of tennis, a vigorous swim, a run, a ride on horseback or a round of golf do not have this effect; but a Long trek, a day of skiing, rowing or cycling or dancing into the small hours usually result in a gain of weight on the following day, unless the patient is in perfect training. In patients coming from abroad, where they always use their cars, we often see this effect after a strenuous day of shopping on foot, sightseeing and visits to galleries and museums. Though the extra muscular effort involved does consume some additional calories, this appears to be offset by the retention of water which the tired circulation cannot at once eliminate.

Appetite-reducing Drugs

We hardly ever use amphetamines, the appetite-reducing drugs such as Dexedrin, Dexamil, Preludin, etc., as there seems to be no need for them during the HCG treatment. The only time we find them useful is when a patient is, for impelling and unforeseen reasons, obliged to forego the injections for three to four days and yet wishes to continue the diet so that he need not interrupt the course.

Unforeseen Interruptions of Treatment

If an interruption of treatment lasting more than four days is necessary, the patient must increase his diet to at least 800 calories by adding meat, eggs, cheese, and milk to his diet after the third day, as otherwise he will find himself so hungry and weak that he is unable to go about his usual occupation. If the interval lasts less than two weeks the patient can directly resume injections and the 500-calorie diet, but if the interruption lasts Longer he must again eat normally until he has had his third injection.

When a patient knows beforehand that he will have to travel and be absent for more than four days, it is always better to stop injections three days before he is due to leave so that he can have the three days of strict dieting which are necessary after the last injection at home. This saves him from the almost impossible task of having to arrange the 500 calorie diet while en route, and he can thus enjoy a much greater dietary freedom from the day of his departure. Interruptions occurring before 20 effective injections have been given are most undesirable, because with less than that number of injections some weight is liable to be regained. After the 20th injection an unavoidable interruption is merely a Loss of time.

Muscular Fatigue

Towards the end of a full course, when a good deal of fat has been rapidly lost, some patients complain that lifting a weight or climbing stairs requires a greater muscular effort than before. They feel neither breathlessness nor exhaustion but simply that their muscles have to work harder. This phenomenon, which disappears soon after the end of the treatment, is caused by the removal of abnormal fat deposited between, in, and around the muscles. The removal of this fat makes the muscles too Long, and so in order to achieve a certain skeletal movement - say the bending of an arm - the muscles have to perform greater contraction than before. Within a short while the muscle adjusts itself perfectly to the new situation, but under HCG the Loss of fat is so rapid that this adjustment cannot keep up with it. Patients often have to be reassured that this does not mean that they are "getting weak". This phenomenon does not occur in patients who regularly take vigorous exercise and continue to do so during treatment.

Massage

I never allow any kind of massage during treatment. It is entirely unnecessary and merely disturbs a very delicate process which is going on in the tissues. Few indeed are the masseurs and masseuses who can resist the temptation to knead and hammer abnormal fat deposits. In the course of rapid reduction it is sometimes possible to pick up a fold of skin which has not yet had time to adjust itself, as it always does under HCG, to the changed figure. This fold contains its normal subcutaneous fat and may be almost an inch thick. It is one of the main objects of the HCG treatment to keep that fat there. Patients and their masseurs do not always understand this and give this fat a working-over. I have seen such patients who were as black and blue as if they had received a sound thrashing.

In my opinion, massage, thumping, rolling, kneading, and shivering undertaken for the purpose of reducing abnormal fat can do nothing but harm. We once had the honor of treating the proprietress of a high class institution that specialized in such antics. She had the audacity to confess that she was taking our treatment to convince her clients of the efficacy of her methods, which she had found useless in her own case.

How anyone in his right mind is able to believe that fatty tissue can be shifted mechanically or be made to vanish by squeezing is beyond my comprehension. The only effect obtained is severe bruising. The torn tissue then forms scars and these slowly contracts making the fatty tissue even harder and more unyielding.

A lady once consulted us for her most ungainly legs. Large masses of fat bulged over the ankles of her tiny feet, and there were about 40 lbs. too much on her hips and thighs. We assured her that this overweight could be lost and that her ankles would markedly improve in the process. Her treatment progressed most satisfactorily but to our surprise there was no improvement in her ankles. We then discovered that she had for years been taking every kind of mechanical, electric and heat treatment for her legs and that she had made up her mind to resort to plastic surgery if we failed.

Re-examining the fat above her ankles, we found that it was unusually hard. We attributed this to the countless minor injuries inflicted by kneading. These injuries had healed but had left a tough network of connective scar-tissue in which the fat was imprisoned. Ready to try anything, she was put to bed for the remaining three weeks of her first course with her Lower legs tightly strapped in unyielding bandages. Every day the pressure was increased. The combination of HCG, diet and strapping brought about a marked improvement in the shape of her ankles. At the end of her first course she returned to her home abroad. Three months later she came back for her second course. She had maintained both her weight and the improvement of her ankles. The same procedure was repeated, and after five weeks she left the hospital with a normal weight and legs that, if not exactly shapely, were at least unobtrusive.

Where no such injuries of the tissues have been inflicted by inappropriate methods of treatment, these drastic measures are never necessary.

Blood Sugar

Towards the end of a course or when a patient has nearly reached his normal weight it occasionally happens that the blood sugar drops below normal, and we have even seen this in patients who had an abnormally high blood sugar before treatment. Such an attack of hypoglycemia is almost identical with the one seen in diabetics who have taken too much insulin. The attack comes on suddenly; there is the same feeling of light-headedness, weakness in the knees, trembling, and unmotivated sweating. But under HCG, hypoglycemia does not produce any feeling of hunger. All these symptoms are almost instantly relieved by taking two heaped teaspoons of sugar.

In the course of treatment the possibility of such an attack is explained to those patients who are in a phase in which a drop in blood sugar may occur. They are instructed to keep sugar or glucose sweets handy, particularly when driving a car. They are also told to watch the effect of taking sugar very carefully and report the following day. This is important, because anxious patients to whom such an attack has been explained are apt to take sugar unnecessarily, in which case it inevitably produces a gain in weight and does not dramatically relieve the symptoms for which it was taken, proving that these were not due to hypoglycemia. Some patients mistake the effects of emotional stress for hypoglycemia. When the symptoms are quickly relieved by sugar this is proof that they were indeed due to an abnormal Lowering of the blood sugar, and in that case there is no increase in the weight on the following day. We always suggest that sugar be taken if the patient is in doubt.

Once such an attack has been relieved with sugar we have never seen it recur on the immediately subsequent days, and only very rarely does a patient have two such attacks separated by several days during a course of treatment. In patients who have not eaten sufficiently during the first two days of treatment we sometimes give sugar when the minor symptoms usually felt during the first three days of treatment continue beyond that time, and in some cases this has seemed to speed up the euphoria ordinarily associated with the HCG method.

The Ratio of Pounds to Inches

An interesting feature of the HCG method is that, regardless of how fat a patient is, the greatest circumference -- abdomen or hips as the case may be is reduced at a constant rate which is extraordinarily close to 1 cm. per kilogram of weight lost. At the beginning of treatment the change in measurements is somewhat greater than this, but at the end of a course it is almost invariably found that the girth is as many centimeters less as the number of kilograms by which the weight has been reduced. I have never seen this clear cut relationship in patients that try to reduce by dieting only.

Preparing the Solution

Human chorionic gonadotrophin comes on the market as a highly soluble powder which is the pure substance extracted from the urine of pregnant women. Such preparations are carefully standardized, and any brand made by a reliable pharmaceutical company is probably as good as any other. The substance should be extracted from the urine and not from the placenta, and it must of course be of human and not of animal origin. The powder is sealed in ampoules or in rubber-capped bottles in varying amounts which are stated in International Units. In this form HCG is stable; however, only such preparations should be used that have the date of manufacture and the date of expiry clearly stated on the label or package. A suitable solvent is always supplied in a separate ampoule in the same package.

Once HCG is in solution it is far less stable. It may be kept at room-temperature for two to three days, but if the solution must be kept longer it should always be refrigerated. When treating only one or two cases simultaneously, vials containing a small number of units say 1000 I.U. should be used. The 10 cc. of solvent which is supplied by the manufacturer is injected into the rubber- capped bottle containing the HCG, and the powder must dissolve instantly. Of this solution 1.25 cc. are withdrawn for each injection. One such bottle of 1000 I.U. therefore furnishes 8 injections. When more than one patient is being treated, they should not each have their own bottle but rather all be injected from the same vial and a fresh solution made when this is empty.

As we are usually treating a fair number of patients at the same time, we prefer to use vials containing 5000 units. With these the manufacturers also supply 10 cc. of solvent. Of such a solution 0.25 cc. contain the 125 I.U., which is the standard dose for all cases and which should never be exceeded. This small amount is awkward to handle accurately (it requires an insulin syringe) and is wasteful, because there is a Loss of solution in the nozzle of the syringe and in the needle. We therefore prefer a higher dilution, which we prepare in the following way: The solvent supplied is injected into the rubber capped bottle containing the 5000 I.U. as these bottles are too small to hold more solvent, we withdraw 5 cc., inject it into an empty rubber-capped bottle and add 5 cc. of normal saline to each bottle. This gives us 10 cc. of solution in each bottle, and of this solution 0.5 cc. contains 125 I.U. This amount is convenient to inject with an ordinary syringe.

Injecting

HCG produces little or no tissue-reaction, it is completely painless and in the many thousands of injections we have given we have never seen an inflammatory or suppurative reaction at the site of the injection.

One should avoid leaving a vacuum in the bottle after preparing the solution or after withdrawal of the amount required for the injections as otherwise alcohol used for sterilizing a frequently perforated rubber cap might be drawn into the solution. When sharp needles are used, it sometimes happens that a little bit of rubber is punched out of the rubber cap and can be seen as a small black speck floating in the solution. As these bits of rubber are heavier than the solution they rapidly settle out, and it is thus easy to avoid drawing them into the syringe.

We use very fine needles that are two inches Long and inject deep intragluteally in the outer upper quadrant of the buttocks. The injection should if possible not be given into the superficial fat layers, which in very obese patients must be compressed so as to enable the needle to reach the muscle. It is also important that the daily injection should be given at intervals as close to 24 hours as possible. Any attempt to economize in time by giving larger doses at longer intervals is doomed to produce less satisfactory results.

There are hardly any contraindications to the HCG method. Treatment can be continued in the presence of abscesses, suppuration, large infected wounds and major fractures. Surgery and general anesthesia are no reason to stop and we have given treatment during a severe attack of malaria. Acne or boils are no contraindication, the former usually clears up, and furunculosis comes to an end. Thrombophlebitis is no contraindication, and we have treated several obese patients with HCG and the 500-calorie diet while suffering from this condition. Our impression has been that in obese patients the phlebitis does rather better and certainly no worse than under the usual treatment alone. This also applies to patients suffering from varicose ulcers which tend to heal rapidly.

Fibroids

While uterine fibroids seem to be in no way affected by HCG in the doses we use, we have found that very large, externally palpable uterine myomas are apt to give trouble. We are convinced that this is entirely due to the rather sudden disappearance of fat from the pelvic bed upon which they rest and that it is the weight of the tumor pressing on the underlying tissues which accounts for the discomfort or pain which may arise during treatment. While we disregard even fair-sized or multiple myomas, we insist that very large ones be operated before treatment. We have had patients present themselves for reducing fat from their abdomen that showed no signs of obesity, but had a large abdominal tumor.

Gallstones

Small stones in the gall bladder may in patients who have recently had typical colics cause more frequent colics under treatment with HCG. This may be due to the almost complete absence of fat from the diet, which prevents the normal emptying of the gall bladder. Before undertaking treatment we explain to such patients that there is a risk of more frequent and possibly severe symptoms and that it may become necessary to operate. If they are prepared to take this risk and provided they agree to undergo an operation if we consider this imperative, we proceed with treatment, as after weight reduction with HCG the operative risk is considerably reduced in an obese patient. In such cases we always give a drug which stimulates the flow of bile, and in the majority of cases nothing untoward happens. On the other hand, we have looked for and not found any evidence to suggest that the HCG treatment leads to the formation of gallstones as pregnancy sometimes does.

The Heart

Disorders of the heart are not as a rule contraindications. In fact, the removal of abnormal fat - particularly from the heart-muscle and from the surrounding of the coronary arteries - can only be beneficial in cases of myocardial weakness, and many such patients are referred to us by cardiologists. Within the first week of treatment all patients - not only heart cases - remark that they have lost much of their breathlessness

Coronary Occlusion

In obese patients who have recently survived a coronary occlusion, we adopt the following procedure in collaboration with the cardiologist. We wait until no further electrocardiographic changes have occurred for a period of three months. Routine treatment is then started under careful control and it is usual to find a further electrocardiographic improvement of a condition which was previously stationary.

In the thousands of cases we have treated we have not once seen any sort of coronary incident occur during or shortly after treatment. The same applies to cerebral vascular accidents. Nor have we ever seen a case of thrombosis of any sort develop during treatment, even though a high blood pressure is rapidly Lowered. In this respect, too, the HCG treatment resembles pregnancy.

Teeth and Vitamins

Patients whose teeth are in poor repair sometimes get more trouble under prolonged treatment, just as may occur in pregnancy. In such cases we do allow calcium and vitamin D, though not in an oily solution. The only other vitamin we permit is vitamin C, which we use in large doses combined with an antihistamine at the onset of a common cold. There is no objection to the use of an antibiotic if this is required, for instance by the dentist. In cases of bronchial asthma and hay fever we have occasionally resorted to cortisone during treatment and find that triamcinolone is the least likely to interfere with the Loss of weight, but many asthmatics improve with HCG alone.

Alcohol

Obese heavy drinkers, even those bordering on alcoholism, often do surprisingly well under HCG and it is exceptional for them to take a drink while under treatment. When they do, they find that a relatively small quantity of alcohol produces intoxication. Such patients say that they do not feel the need to drink. This may in part be due to the euphoria which the treatment produces and in part to the complete absence of the need for quick sustenance from which most obese patients suffer.

Though we have had a few cases that have continued abstinence long after treatment, others relapse as soon as they are back on a normal diet. We have a few "regular customers" who, having once been reduced to their normal weight, start to drink again though watching their weight. Then after some months they purposely overeat in order to gain sufficient weight for another course of HCG which temporarily gets them out of their drinking routine. We do not particularly welcome such cases, but we see no reason for refusing their request.

Tuberculosis

It is interesting that obese patients suffering from inactive pulmonary tuberculosis can be safely treated. We have under very careful control treated patients as early as three months after they were pronounced inactive and have never seen a relapse occur during or shortly after treatment. In fact, we only have one case on our records in which active tuberculosis developed in a young man about one year after a treatment which had lasted three weeks. Earlier X-rays showed a calcified spot from a childhood infection which had not produced clinical symptoms. There was a family history of tuberculosis, and his illness started under adverse conditions which certainly had nothing to do with the treatment. Residual calcifications from an early infection are exceedingly common, and we never consider them a contraindication to treatment.

The Painful Heel

In obese patients who have been trying desperately to keep their weight down by severe dieting, a curious symptom sometimes occurs. They complain of an unbearable pain in their heels which they feel only while standing or walking. As soon as they take the weight off their heels the pain ceases. These cases are the bane of the rheumatologists and orthopedic surgeons who have treated them before they come to us. All the usual investigations are entirely negative, and there is not the slightest response to anti-rheumatic medication or physiotherapy. The pain may be so severe that the patients are obliged to give up their occupation, and they are not infrequently labeled as a case of hysteria. When their heels are carefully examined one finds that the sole is softer than normal and that the heel bone - the calcaneus - can be distinctly felt, which is not the case in a normal foot.

We interpret the condition as a lack of the hard fatty pad on which the calcaneus rests and which protects both the bone and the skin of the sole from pressure. This fat is like a springy cushion which carries the weight of the body. Standing on a heel in which this fat is missing or reduced must obviously be very painful. In their efforts to keep their weight down these patients have consumed this normal structural fat.

Those patients who have a normal or subnormal weight while showing the typically obese fat deposits are made to eat to capacity, often much against their will, for one week. They gain weight rapidly but there is no improvement in the painful heels. They are then started on the routine HCG treatment. Overweight patients are treated immediately. In both cases the pain completely disappears in 10-20 days of dieting, usually around the 15th day of treatment, and so far no case has had a relapse. We have been able to follow up such patients for years.

We are particularly interested in these cases, as they furnish further proof of the contention that HCG + 500 calories not only removes abnormal fat but actually permits normal fat to be replaced, in spite of the deficient food intake. It is certainly not so that the mere Loss of weight reduces the pain, because it frequently disappears before the weight the patient had prior to the period of forced feeding is reached.

The Skeptical Patient

Any doctor who starts using the HCG method for the first time will have considerable difficulty, particularly if he himself is not fully convinced, in making patients believe that they will not feel hungry on 500 calories and that their face will not collapse. New patients always anticipate the phenomena they know so well from previous treatments and diets and are incredulous when told that these will not occur. We overcome all this by letting new patients spend a little time in the waiting room with older hands, who can always be relied upon to allay these fears with evangelistic zeal, often demonstrating the finer points on their own body.

A waiting-room filled with obese patients who congregate daily is a sort of group therapy. They compare notes and pop back into the waiting room after the consultation to announce the score of the last 24 hours to an enthralled audience. They cross-check on their diets and sometimes confess sins which they try to hide from us, usually with the result that the patient in whom they have confided palpitatingly tattles the whole disgraceful story to us with a "But don't let her know I told you."

Concluding a Course

When the three days of dieting after the last injection are over, the patients are told that they may now eat anything they please, except sugar and starch provided they faithfully observe one simple rule. This rule is that they must have their own portable bathroom-scale always at hand, particularly while traveling. They must without fail weight themselves every morning as they get out of bed, having first emptied their bladder. If they are in the habit of having breakfast in bed, they must weigh before breakfast.

It takes about 3 weeks before the weight reached at the end of the treatment becomes stable, i.e. does not show violent fluctuations after an occasional excess. During this period patients must realize that the so-called carbohydrates, that are sugar, rice, bread, potatoes, pastries etc, are by far the most dangerous. If no carbohydrates whatsoever are eaten, fats can be indulged in somewhat more liberally and even small quantities of alcohol, such as a glass of wine with meals, does no harm, but **as soon as fats and starch are combined things are very liable to get out of hand.** This has to be observed very carefully during the first 3 weeks after the treatment is ended otherwise disappointments are almost sure to occur.

Skipping a Meal

As Long as their weight stays within two pounds of the weight reached on the day of the last injection, patients should take no notice of any increase but the moment the scale goes beyond two pounds, even if this is only a few ounces, they must on that same day entirely skip breakfast and lunch but take plenty to drink. In the evening they must eat a huge steak with only an apple or a raw tomato. Of course this rule applies only to the morning weight. Ex-obese patients should never check their weight during the day, as there may be wide fluctuations and these are merely alarming and confusing.

It is of utmost importance that the meal is skipped on the same day as the scale registers an increase of more than two pounds and that missing the meals is not postponed until the following day. If a meal is skipped on the day in which a gain is registered in the morning this brings about an immediate drop of often over a pound. But if the skipping of the meal - and skipping means literally skipping, not just having a light meal - is postponed the phenomenon does not occur and several days of strict dieting may be necessary to correct the situation.

Most patients hardly ever need to skip a meal. If they have eaten a heavy lunch they feel no desire to eat their dinner, and in this case no increase takes place. If they keep their weight at the point reached at the end of the treatment, even a heavy dinner does not bring about an increase of two pounds on the next morning and does not therefore call for any special measures. Most patients are surprised how small their appetite has become and yet how much they can eat without gaining weight. They no Longer suffer from an abnormal appetite and feel satisfied with much less food than before. In fact, they are usually disappointed that they cannot manage their first normal meal, which they have been planning for weeks.

Losing more Weight

An ex-patient should never gain more than two pounds without immediately correcting this, but it is equally undesirable that more than two lbs. be lost after treatment, because a greater Loss is always achieved at the expense of normal fat. Any normal fat that is lost is invariably regained as soon as more food is taken, and it often happens that this rebound overshoots the upper two lbs. limit.

Trouble After Treatment

Two difficulties may be encountered in the immediate post-treatment period. When a patient has consumed all his abnormal fat or, when after a full course, the injection has temporarily lost its efficacy owing to the body having gradually evolved a counter regulation, the patient at once begins to feel much more hungry and even weak. In spite of repeated warnings, some over-enthusiastic patients do not report this. However, in about two days the fact that they are being undernourished becomes visible in their faces, and treatment is then stopped at once. In such cases - and only in such cases - we allow a very slight increase in the diet, such as an extra apple, 150 grams of meat or two or three extra breadsticks during the three days of dieting after the last injection.

When abnormal fat is no Longer being put into circulation either because it has been consumed or because immunity has set in, this is always felt by the patient as sudden, intolerable and constant hunger. In this sense, the HCG method is completely self-limiting. With HCG it is impossible to reduce a patient, however enthusiastic, beyond his normal weight. As soon as no more abnormal fat is being issued, the body starts consuming normal fat, and this is always regained as soon as ordinary feeding is resumed. The patient then finds that the 2-3 lbs. he has lost during the last days of treatment are immediately regained. A meal is skipped and maybe a pound is lost. The next day this pound is regained, in spite of a careful watch over the food intake. In a few days a tearful patient is back in the consulting room, convinced that her case is a failure.

All that is happening is that the essential fat lost at the end of the treatment, owing to the patient's reluctance to report a much greater hunger, is being replaced. The weight at which such a patient must stabilize thus lies 2-3 lbs. higher than the weight reached at the end of the treatment. Once this higher basic level is established, further difficulties in controlling the weight at the new point of stabilization hardly arise.

Beware of Over-enthusiasm

The other trouble which is frequently encountered immediately after treatment is again due to over-enthusiasm. Some patients cannot believe that they can eat fairly normally without regaining weight. They disregard the advice to eat anything they please except sugar and starch and want to play safe. They try more or less to continue the 500-calorie diet on which they felt so well during treatment and make only minor variations, such as replacing the meat with an egg, cheese, or a glass of milk. To their horror they find that in spite of this bravura, their weight goes up. So, following instructions, they skip one meager lunch and at night eat only a little salad and drink a pot of unsweetened tea, becoming increasingly hungry and weak. The next morning they find that they have increased yet another pound. They feel terrible, and even the dreaded swelling of their ankles is back. Normally we check our patients one week after they have been eating freely, but these cases return in a few days. Either their eyes are filled with tears or they angrily imply that when we told them to eat normally we were just fooling them.

Protein deficiency

Here too, the explanation is quite simple. During treatment the patient has been only just above the verge of protein deficiency and has had the advantage of protein being fed back into his system from the breakdown of fatty tissue. Once the treatment is over there is no more HCG in the body and this process no Longer takes place. Unless an adequate amount of protein is eaten as soon as the treatment is over, protein deficiency is bound to develop, and this inevitably causes the marked retention of water known as hunger-edema.

The treatment is very simple. The patient is told to eat two eggs for breakfast and a huge steak for lunch and dinner followed by a large helping of cheese and to phone through the weight the next morning. When these instructions are followed a stunned voice is heard to report that two lbs. have vanished overnight, that the ankles are normal but that sleep was disturbed, owing to an extraordinary need to pass large quantities of water. The patient having learned this lesson usually has no further trouble.

Relapses

As a general rule one can say that 60%-70% of our cases experience little or no difficulty in holding their weight permanently. Relapses may be due to negligence in the basic rule of daily weighing. Many patients think that this is unnecessary and that they can judge any increase from the fit of their clothes. Some do not carry their scale with them on a journey as it is cumbersome and takes a big bite out of their luggage-allowance when flying. This is a disastrous mistake, because after a course of HCG as much as 10 lbs. can be regained without any noticeable change in the fit of the clothes. The reason for this is that after treatment newly acquired fat is at first evenly distributed and does not show the former preference for certain parts of the body.

Pregnancy or the menopause may annul the effect of a previous treatment. Women who take treatment during the one year after the last menstruation - that is at the onset of the menopause - do just as well as others, but among them the relapse rate is higher until the menopause is fully established. The period of one year after the last menstruation applies only to women who are not being treated with ovarian hormones. If these are taken, the premenopausal period may be indefinitely prolonged.

Late teenage girls who suffer from attacks of compulsive eating have by far the worst record of all as far as relapses are concerned.

Patients who have once taken the treatment never seem to hesitate to come back for another short course as soon as they notice that their weight is once again getting out of hand. They come quite cheerfully and hopefully, assured that they can be helped again. Repeat courses are often even more satisfactory than the first treatment and have the advantage, as do second courses that the patient already knows that he will feel comfortable throughout.

Plan of a Normal Course

125 I.U. of HCG daily (except during menstruation) injections have been given.

Until 3rd injection forced feeding.

After 3rd injection, 500 calorie diet to be continued until 72 hours after the last injection.

For the following 3 weeks, all foods allowed except starch and sugar in any form (careful with very sweet fruit).

After 3 weeks, very gradually add starch in small quantities, always controlled by morning weighing.

CONCLUSION

The HCG + diet method can bring relief to every case of obesity, but the method is not simple. It is very time consuming and requires perfect cooperation between physician and patient. Each case must be handled individually, and the physician must have time to answer questions, allay fears and remove misunderstandings. He must also check the patient daily. When something goes wrong he must at once investigate until he finds the reason for any gain that may have occurred. In most cases it is useless to hand the patient a diet-sheet and let the nurse give him a "shot."

The method involves a highly complex bodily mechanism, and the physician must make himself some sort of picture of what is actually happening; otherwise he will not be able to deal with such difficulties as may arise during treatment.

I must beg those trying the method for the first time to adhere very strictly to the technique and the interpretations here outlined and thus treat a few hundred cases before embarking on experiments of their own, and until then refrain from introducing innovations, however thrilling they may seem. In a new method, innovations or departures from the original technique can only be usefully evaluated against a substantial background of experience with what is at the moment the orthodox procedure.

I have tried to cover all the problems that come to my mind. Yet a bewildering array of new questions keeps arising, and my interpretations are still fluid. In particular, I have never had an opportunity of conducting the laboratory investigations which are so necessary for a theoretical understanding of clinical observations, and I can only hope that those more fortunately placed will in time be able to fill this gap.

The problems of obesity are perhaps not so dramatic as the problems of cancer, but they often cause life Long suffering. How many promising careers have been ruined by excessive fat; how many lives have been shortened. If some way - however cumbersome - can be found to cope effectively with this universal problem of modern civilized man, our world will be a happier place for countless fellowmen and women.

GLOSSARY

ACNE . . . Common skin disease in which pimples, often containing pus, appear on face, neck and shoulders.

ACTH . . . Abbreviation for adrenocorticotrophic hormone. One of the many hormones produced by the anterior lobe of the pituitary gland. ACTH controls the outer part, rind or cortex of the adrenal glands. When ACTH is injected it dramatically relieves arthritic pain, but it has many undesirable side effects, among which is a condition similar to severe obesity. ACTH is now usually replaced by cortisone.

ADRENALIN . . . Hormone produced by the inner part of the Adrenals. Among many other functions, adrenalin is concerned with blood pressure, emotional stress, fear and cold.

ADRENALS . . . Endocrine glands. Small bodies situated atop the kidneys and hence also known as suprarenal glands. The adrenals have an outer rind or cortex which produces vitally important hormones, among which are Cortisone similar substances. The adrenal cortex is controlled by ACTH. The inner part of the adrenals, the medulla, secretes adrenalin and is chiefly controlled by the autonomous nervous system.

ADRENOCORTEX... See adrenals.

AMPHETAMINES . . . Synthetic drugs which reduce the awareness of hunger and stimulate mental activity, rendering sleep impossible. When used for the latter two purposes they are dangerously habit-forming. They do not diminish the body's need for food, but merely suppress the perception of that need. The original drug was known as Benzedrine, from which modern variants such as Dexedrine, Dexamil, and Preludin have been derived. Amphetamines may help an obese patient to prevent a further increase in weight but are unsatisfactory for reducing, as they do not cure the underlying disorder and as their prolonged use may lead to malnutrition and addiction.

ARTERIOSCLEROSIS . . . Hardening of the arterial wall through the calcification of abnormal deposits of a fatlike substance known as cholesterol.

ASCHFIEIM-ZONDEK . . . Authors of a test by which early pregnancy can be diagnosed by injecting a woman's urine into female mice. The HCG present in pregnancy urine produces certain changes in the vagina of these animals. Many similar tests, using other animals such as rabbits, frogs, etc. have been devised.

ASSIMILATE . . . Absorbed digested food from the intestines.

AUTONOMOUS . . . Here used to describe the independent or vegetative nervous system which manages the automatic regulations of the body.

BASAL METABOLISM . . . The body's chemical turnover at complete rest and when fasting. The basal metabolic rate is expressed as the amount of oxygen used up in a given time. The basal metabolic rate (BMR) is controlled by the thyroid gland.

CALORIE . . . The physicist's calorie is the amount of heat required to raise the temperature of 1 cc. of water by 1 degree Centigrade. **The dietician's Calorie (always written with a capital C) is 1000 times greater.** Thus when we speak of a 500 Calorie diet this means that the body is being supplied with as much fuel as would be required to raise the temperature of 500 liters of water by 1 degree Centigrade or 50 liters by 10 degrees. This is quite insufficient to cover the heat and energy requirements of an adult body. In the HCG method the deficit is made up from the abnormal fat-deposits, of which **1 lb. furnishes the body with more than 2000 calories.** As this is roughly the amount lost every day, a patient under HCG is never short of fuel.

CEREBRAL . . . Of the brain. Cerebral vascular disease is a disorder concerning the blood vessels of the brain, such as cerebral thrombosis or hemorrhage, known as apoplexy or stroke.

CHOLESTEROL . . . A fatlike substance contained in almost every cell of the body. In the blood it exists in two forms, known as free and esterified. The latter form is under certain conditions deposited in the inner lining of the arteries (see arteriosclerosis). No clear and definite relationship between fat intake and cholesterol-level in the blood has yet been established.

CHORIONIC . . . Of the chorion, which is part of the placenta or after-birth. The term chorionic is justly applied to HCG, as this hormone is exclusively produced in the placenta, from where it enters the human mother's blood and is later excreted in her urine.

COMPULSIVE EATING. . . A form of oral gratification with which a repressed sex-instinct is sometimes vicariously relieved. Compulsive eating must not be confused with the real hunger from which most obese patients suffer.

CONGENITAL . . . Any condition which exists at or before birth.

CORONARY ARTERIES . . . Two blood vessels which encircle the heart and supply all the blood required by the heart-muscle.

CORPUS LUTEUM . . . A yellow body which forms in the ovary at the follicle from which an egg has been detached. This body acts as an endocrine gland and plays an important role in menstruation and pregnancy. Its secretion is one of the sex hormones, and it is stimulated by another hormone known as LSH, which stands for luteum stimulating hormones. LSH is produced in the anterior lobe of the pituitary gland. LSH is truly gonadotrophic and must never be confused with HCG, which is a totally different substance, having no direct action on the corpus luteum.

CORTEX . . . Outer covering or rind. The term is applied to the outer part of the adrenals but is also used to describe the gray matter which covers the white matter of the brain.

CORTISONE . . . A synthetic substance which acts like an adrenal hormone. It is today used in the treatment of a large number of illnesses, and several chemical variants have been produced, among which are prednisone and Triamcinolone.

CUSHING . . . A great American brain surgeon who described a condition of extreme obesity associated with symptoms of adrenal disorder. Cushing's Syndrome may be caused by organic disease of the pituitary or the adrenal glands but, as was later discovered, it also occurs as a result of excessive ACTH medication.

DIENCEPHALON . . . A primitive and hence very old part of the brain which lies between and under the two large hemispheres. In man the diencephalon (or hypothalamus) is subordinate to the higher brain or cortex, and yet it ultimately controls all that happens inside the body. It regulates all the endocrine glands, the autonomous nervous system, the turnover of fat and sugar. It seems also to be the seat of the primitive animal instincts and is the relay station at which emotions are translated into bodily reactions.

DIURETIC. . . . Any substance that increases the flow of urine.

DYSFUNCTION . . . Abnormal functioning of any organ, be this excessive, deficient or in any way altered.

EDEMA . . . An abnormal accumulation of water in the tissues.

ELECTROCARDIOGRAM . . . Tracing of electric phenomena taking place in the heart during each beat. The tracing provides information about the condition and working of the heart which is not otherwise obtainable.

ENDOCRINE . . . We distinguish endocrine and exocrine glands. The former produce hormones, chemical regulators, which they secrete directly into the blood circulation in the gland and from where they are carried all over the body. Examples of endocrine glands are the pituitary, the thyroid and the adrenals. Exocrine glands produce a visible secretion such as saliva, sweat, urine. There are also glands which are endocrine and exocrine. Examples are the testicles, the prostate and the pancreas, which produces the hormone insulin and digestive ferments which flow from the gland into the intestinal tract. Endocrine glands are closely inter-dependent of each other, they are linked to the autonomous nervous system and the diencephalon presides over this whole incredibly complex regulatory system.

EMACIATED . . . Grossly undernourished.

EUPHORIA . . . A feeling of particular physical and mental well-being.

FERAL . . . Wild, unrestrained.

FIBROID . . . Any benign new growth of connective tissue. When such a tumor originates from a muscle, it is known as a myoma. The most common seat of myomas is the uterus.

FOLLICLE . . . Any small bodily cyst or sac containing a liquid. Here the term applies to the ovarian cyst in which the egg is formed. The egg is expelled when a ripe follicle bursts and this is known as ovulation (see corpus luteum).

FSH . . . Abbreviation for follicle-stimulating hormone. FSH is another (see corpus luteum) anterior pituitary hormone which acts directly on the ovarian follicle and is therefore correctly called a gonadotrophin.

GLANDS . . . See endocrine.

GONADOTROPHIN . . . See corpus luteum, follicle and FSH. Gonadotrophic literally means sex gland-directed. FSH, LSH and the equivalent hormones in the male, all produced in the anterior Lobe of the pituitary gland, are true gonadotrophins. Unfortunately and confusingly, the term gonadotrophin has also been applied to the placental hormone of pregnancy known as human chorionic gonadotrophin (HCG). This hormone acts on the diencephalon and can only indirectly influence the sex-glands via the anterior Lobe of the pituitary.

HCG . . . Abbreviation for human chorionic gonadotrophin

HORMONES . . . See endocrine.

HYPERTENSION . . . High blood pressure.

HYPOGLYCEMIA . . . A condition in which the blood sugar is below normal. It can be relieved by eating sugar.

HYPOPHYSIS . . . Another name for the pituitary gland.

HYPOTHESIS . . . A tentative explanation or speculation on how observed facts and isolated scientific data can be brought into an intellectually satisfying relationship of cause and effect. Hypotheses are useful for directing further research, but they are not necessarily an exposition of what is believed to be the truth. Before a hypothesis can advance to the dignity of a theory or a law, it must be confirmed by all future research. As soon as research turns up data which no Longer fit the hypothesis, it is immediately abandoned for a better one.

LSH . . . See corpus luteum.

METABOLISM . . . See basal metabolism.

MIGRAINE . . . Severe half-sided headache often associated with vomiting.

MUCOID . . . Slime-like.

MYOCARDIUM . . . The heart-muscle.

MYOMA . . . See fibroid.

MYXEDEMA . . . Accumulation of a mucoid substance in the tissues which occurs in cases of severe primary thyroid deficiency.

NEOLITHIC . . . In the history of human culture we distinguish the Early Stone Age or Paleolithic, the Middle Stone Age or Mesolithic and the New Stone Age or Neolithic period. The Neolithic period started about 8000 years ago when the first attempts at agriculture, pottery and animal domestication made at the end of the Mesolithic period suddenly began to develop rapidly along the road that led to modern civilization.

NORMAL SALINE . . . A low concentration of salt in water equal to the salinity of body fluids.

PHLEBITIS . . . An inflammation of the veins. When a blood-clot forms at the site of the inflammation, we speak of Thrombophlebitis.

PITUITARY . . . A very complex endocrine gland which lies at the base of the skull, consisting chiefly of an anterior and a posterior lobe. The pituitary is controlled by the diencephalon, which regulates the anterior Lobe by means of hormones which reach it through small blood vessels. The posterior Lobe is controlled by nerves which run from the diencephalon into this part of the gland. The anterior Lobe secretes many hormones, among which are those that regulate other glands such as the thyroid, the adrenals and the sex glands.

PLACENTA . . . The after-birth. In women, a large and highly complex organ through which the child in the womb receives its nourishment from the mother's body. It is the organ in which HCG is manufactured and then given off into the mother's blood.

PROTEIN . . . The living substance in plant and animal cells. Herbivorous animals can thrive on plant protein alone, but man must base some protein of animal origin (milk, eggs or flesh) to live healthily. When insufficient protein is eaten, the body retains water.

PSORIASIS . . . A skin disease which produces scaly patches. These tend to disappear during pregnancy and during the treatment of obesity by the HCG method.

RENAL . . . Of the kidney.

RESERPINE . . . An Indian drug extensively used in the treatment of high blood pressure and some forms of mental disorder.

RETENTION ENEMA . . . The slow infusion of a liquid into the rectum, from where it is absorbed and not evacuated.

SACRUM . . . A fusion of the Lower vertebrate into the large bony mass to which the pelvis is attached.

SEDIMENTATION RATE . . . The speed at which a suspension of red blood cells settles out. A rapid settling out is called a high sedimentation rate and may be indicative of a large number of bodily disorders of pregnancy.

SEXUAL SELECTION . . . A sexual preference for individuals which show certain traits. If this preference or selection goes on generation after generation, more and more individuals showing the trait will appear among the general population. The natural environment has little or nothing to do with this process. Sexual selection therefore differs from natural selection, to which modern man is no Longer subject because he changes his environment rather than let the environment change him.

STRIATION . . . Tearing of the Lower layers of the skin owing to rapid stretching in obesity or during pregnancy. When first formed striae are dark reddish lines which later change into white scars.

SUPRARENAL GLANDS . . . See adrenals.

SYNDROME . . . A group of symptoms which in their association are characteristic of a particular disorder.

THROMBOPHLEBITIS . . . See phlebitis.

THROMBUS . . . A blood-clot in a blood-vessel.

TRIAMCINOLOWNE . . . A modern derivative of cortisone.

URIC ACID . . . A product of incomplete protein-breakdown or utilization in the body. When uric acid becomes deposited in the gristle of the joints we speak of gout.

VARICOSE ULCERS . . . Chronic ulceration above the ankles due to varicose veins which interfere with the normal blood circulation in the affected areas.

VEGETATIVE . . . See autonomous.

VERTEBRATE . . . Any animal that has a back-bone.

Beth Golden

Made in the USA
Charleston, SC
02 April 2014